THE P...
HANDBOOK

The catalogue of gambling books, videos and software

Year 2001 edition

Edited by Scott Eldred and Ion Mills

High Stakes

High Stakes Bookshop
21 Great Ormond Street
London WC1N 3JB
T 020 7430 1021
F 020 7430 0021
info@highstakes.co.uk
www.highstakes.co.uk

Published by High Stakes Publishing
18 Coleswood Rd, Harpenden, Herts, AL5 1EQ

1 874061 05 X

Printed by Omnia, Glasgow

CONTENTS

Introduction

A quicker updated new edition of The Punter's Handbook this time with an even bigger range of books, videos, software and gambling paraphernalia.

Books are listed in the catalogue by subject and product number, higher numbers usually mean that the book is newer or we have only just discovered it!

We are still (subject to a rent review!!) at 21 Great Ormond Street, London WC1N 3JB - just down the road from the famous children's hospital and we are still the only specialist retail gambling bookshop in the UK. Scott Eldred (ex-Sportspages) is the manager and the shop is open Monday to Friday 11.00 to 6.00.
We have a wide range of titles in stock at all times, plus some books, special offers, videos and software not listed in this catalogue. We are in the process of improving our service from the US to enable us to get an even wider range of products, quicker.
We are also planning to start taking in second-hand titles, especially Poker books, so if you have books you would like to get rid of — call Scott on 020 7430 1021 or e-mail him at scott@highstakes.co.uk.

We can be contacted on 020 7430 1021 (Tel), 020 7430 0021 (Fax) and by e-mail: info@highstakes.co.uk Nearest underground stations are Russell Square (Piccadilly Line) and Holborn (Piccadilly and Central Line).

The website at **www.highstakes.co.uk** is up and running and you can securely order all your gambling books online, anytime, any day.

We accept Visa, MasterCard, Switch and Connect credit/debit cards. We only debit your card when the goods are dispatched.
Cheques should be in pounds sterling and drawn on a UK bank, payable to High Stakes. UK Postal orders are accepted.
Shipping costs work out at £1.95 plus 50p a book for UK orders (usually 2nd class post) and £2.95 plus £1 a book elsewhere (usually Printed Mail). If you require books more urgently please contact us for a quote for the postage.

Security - Under no circumstances do we rent out our customer lists to third parties, although we might include information from other companies in our mailings that we think would be of interest to you.

If you have any queries, complaints, suggestions please get in touch with us at the shop and we will endeavour to help you.

RECENT ARRIVALS

g1655, **On Tilt – A Diary of a Spread Better**, Iain Fletcher, £9.99pb, 90pp, Iain Fletcher was given a £6,000 spend-as-you-like trading account with Sporting Index any profit he made in twelve months was his to keep. This is (auto)biography mixed with sensible advice in a real life betting situations. It helps that the author can write well, be entertaining and the subject matter is gambling on British sports such as Rugby, Cricket, Soccer and Horse Racing. Anyone who has ever fancied being a full time gambling pro, those of us who dream it and anyone interested in making money spread betting - should read this terrific account of a year as professional spread better

G1656, **Starting Out in Poker**, Stewart Reuben, £9.99pb, In this user-friendly introduction to the game, professional player and Poker teacher Stewart Reuben provides newcomers to the game with a thorough grounding in the essentials of play. All the popular variants of Poker are discussed

G1658, **The Compleat Horseplayer**, David Edelman, £19.95pb, 100pp, An important and valuable book including : Elements, Odds, Markets, Value, information, Money Management, Staking and the Bank Concept, Kelly and Quasi – Kelly Staking, Betting Markets, Technical Analysis, Technical Versus Fundamental Analysis, Arbitrage, Hidden Information, Bookmaker vs. TOTE, Fluctuations, Exotics: About Boxing, Technical Analysis – Methodology, Fundamental Analysis in Racing, Class, Empirical Class ratings Models, Beyer-like Speed ratings, Weight, Fitness, Mudrunners, Red Herrings, Statistical Modeling and much more

G1659, **Bias 2001**, A Renham, £10.00 manuscript, 74pp, This book aims to give you information that will keep you one step ahead of the bookies. It deals with two vital factors in British flat racing - the class of a horse, (focusing on handicap races), and the importance of where a horse is drawn. Both are discussed in detail

G1662, **Racehorses of 2001**, Timeform, £69.00hb, 1183pp, Covers every horse that has run during the British flat racing year with extended essays on the leading performers. Every horse is given its own individual Timeform rating and commentary

G1664, **Sun Guide to the Flat 2001**, £4.99pb, 160pp, Includes Horses to Follow in 2001, 50 Dark Horses and Top Stable Secrets

G1674, **Telling Lies and Getting Paid**, Michael Konik, £21.95hb, 241pp, This is a sequel to the well received Man with the $100,000 Breasts, Michael Konik again goes behind the scenes and into the action of the fascinating world of risk and reward. Among the essays is the Chicago Nun who consistently out-handicaps the bookies with her pro football picks

G1677, **Two Year Olds of 2001**, Steve Taplin, £6.99pb, 281pp, Seventeenth edition of Steve Taplin's in-depth assessments of the 1,200 or so unraced two-year olds

G1678 **The Solidus**, Davey Towey, £17.95 pb, 96pp, Horse racing system to assess distance, going, weight and class. Originally available at £25

G1663 **Profile (Racehorses and Sires)** - Flat Edition 2001. £19.95 pb, 470pp, A four year analysis of racehorse performances covering every horse that ran last season and gained a win the in the last 4 seasons

SPECIAL OFFERS

Visit our web-site www.highstakes.co.uk to see our weekly updated special offers. Below are permanent catalogue 2001 special offers please quote relevant code when placing your order

GSO1514 **Football Betting to Win**, Jacques Black Was £9.99 now £7.99

GSO36 **Hold'em Poker for Advanced Players** – David Sklansky Was £29.95 now £24.95

GSO465 **Theory of Poker** – David Sklansky Was £29.95 now £24.95

GSO841 **Winner's Guide to Texas Holdem** – Ken Warren Was £14.95 now £12.00

GSO911 **Better One Day as a Lion** – Raymond Smith Was £9.95 now £4.95

YEAR 2000 BEST-SELLERS

1. FOOTBALL BETTING TO WIN – JACQUES BLACK

2. ESSENTIAL FOOTBALL BETTING GUIDE – PAUL STEELE

3. HOLD'EM POKER FOR ADVANCED PLAYERS – DAVID SKLANSY

4. SUPER/SYSTEM – DOYLE BRUNSON

5. FOOTBALL FORTUNES – BILL HUNTER

6. POT-LIMIT & NO-LIMIT POKER – STEWART REUBEN

7. OMAHA HOLDEM POKER – BOB CIAFFONE

8. HOLDEM POKER – DAVID SKLANSKY

9. THE THEORY OF POKER – DAVID SKLANSKY

10. SPREAD BETTING TO WIN – JACQUES BLACK

BACCARAT

g196, **Baccarat Fair And Foul**, Professor Hoffman, £2.95pb, 62pp, An explanation of the game and a warning against its dangers! First published in 1891., US Book

g225, **Facts Of Baccarat**, Walter Nolan, £1.50pb, 46pp, Basic booklet. An introduction., US Book

g678, **Winning Baccarat Strategies**, Henry Tamburin, £19.95pb, 85pp, Covers basics then Systems, Money Management, The Computer SEZ Game, ESP, Rating the Cards etc. Recommended, US Book

g976, **John Patricks Baccarat**, John Patrick, £18.95pb, 246pp, How to play and win at the table with the fastest action and the highest stakes, US Book

g1140, **Baccarat For The Clueless**, John May, £12pb, 144pp, Covers: History, Card Counting, Analysing the Shuffle, Cheating, The Internet, Psychology and more. For beginners up to more serious players., US Book

g1372, **Baccarat Battle Book**: How to Attack Baccarat & Mini-Baccarat, Frank Scoblete, £12.95pb, 214pp, The most elegant game in the casino can also be one of the most deadly for unwary and unwise players. Baccarat and mini-baccarat have some of the lowest house edges of any casino games. Yet one is player-friendly and one is player-deadly. Find out which is which and why!. Frank show players how to push the house to reduce the casino's commission on the Bank bet from five percent to four percent. Show how manipulating the pace of the game can bring more comps for less risk. He also explains and analyses many of the most famous betting systems and shows why they leave much to be desired. Then he shows how to utilize his special variations of these systems to reduce the player's exposure to the house edge. Frank describes the Seven Deadly Sins of Gambling and how to avoid them. Finally, Frank describes his 13 Baccarat Battle rules for Successful Play., US Book

g1416, **Power Baccarat 2**, Byron F.Herbert , £19.95pb, 287pp, New techniques and strategies that are sure to carry players to the next level of expertise, US Book

g1502, **Baccarat Made Simple**, David Vernon, £9.95pb, 30pp, A unique approach to teach a novice the game including rules, the shoe thoroughly explained and numerous charts, US Book

g1594, **Lyle Stuart on Baccarat**, Lyle Stuart, £20pb, 302pp, Updated version of his 1984 bestseller. Advice and autobiographical detail combine in this popular book., US Book

BACKGAMMON

g439, **Backgammon For Winners**, Bill Robertie, £9.95pb, 131pp, For beginners to intermediate. Easy to read, informative and illustrated, US Book

g1174, **Backgammon For Serious Players**, Bill Robertie, £14.95pb, 200pp, Includes 5 actual games. Learn to play boldly, build primes quickly, go for gammons, killing numbers, doubling in the opening, duplication, creating shots, and more, US Book

g1254, **Backgammon: An Independent View**, Chris Bray, £11.99pb, 127pp, A collection of articles culled from Bray's column in the Independent where he has been writing about backgammon for over four years , UK Book

g1258, **Backgammon**, Paul Magriel, £45pb, 402pp, One of the most important books ever written on the game. 5 sections covering: Basics, Using Men Effectively, Middle Game Strategy, Endgame, and Advanced Positional Play Recommended, US Book

g1332, **100 Backgammon Puzzles**, Paul Lamford, £4.99pb, 126pp, This book contains 100 fascinating and testing backgammon puzzles which can be enjoyed without setting up a board. Half are decisions on checker plays and half are decisions on whether to double and whether to accept an offered cube, UK Book

g1471, **Discovering Backgammon**, R.C. Bell, £3.5pb, 48pp, This book is intended to help new players to master the fundamentals of the game, UK Book

g1476, **Know the Game: Backgammon**, G.I.A Titley, £4.99pb, 48pp, This accessible and comprehensive guide describes all aspects of backgammon, from setting up the board to the complex strategy of the back game. Both beginner and competent player will find its concise explanation of the arithmetic and the various odds especially useful in improving the standard of play., UK Book

g1592, **501 Essential Backgammon Problems**, Bill Robertie, £19.95pb, 384pp, A complete approach, 31 chapters cover every part of the game, from the opening roll to the art of endgame settlements. You'll learn when to attack blots, how to master the blitz, and about anchors, primes, crunched positions, mastering a race, calculating bearoffs, the back game, checker play problems, doubling and much more, UK Book

BLACKJACK

g16, Winning Blackjack Without Counting Cards, David S Popik, £8.99pb, 104pp, For use against eight decks, this is for casuals and experts who don't wish to count. Offers a basic strategy which must be observed , US Book

g18, Playing Blackjack as a Business, Lawrence Revere, £16.95pb, 177pp, One of the finest books written on the subject, by the ruthless professional player Revere, who won consistently for a long time, without being banned, US Book

g24, Beat The Dealer, Edward Thorp, £10pb, 204pp, A classic, first published in 1962, the original blackjack basic strategy improved upon over the years but still invaluable to the novice and intermediate player, US Book

g81, John Patrick's Blackjack, John Patrick, £15.95pb, 193pp, In this you'll learn about The Big 4 - Bankroll, Knowledge, Money Management, and Discipline - the heart and soul of JP's winning programme, US Book

g82, Blackjack: A Winner's Handbook, Jerry Patterson, £10.95pb, 250pp, Includes shuffle tracking, three counting techniques, a unique four phase non-count strategy, a seven-step winning programme and much more besides, US Book

g85, Beginners Guide to Winning Blackjack, Stanley Roberts, £9.95pb, 241pp, For beginners up to the more experienced; shows how to win whether one, two or four decks are being used, US Book

g89, Ken Uston on Blackjack, Ken Uston, £12.95pb, 212pp, A memoir about Uston's personal battle with casino's over the years;how they banned him and how he thought up systems to beat them. Uston is now sadly deceased, US Book

g101, Million Dollar Blackjack, Ken Uston, £18.95pb, 327pp, Uston packed in a high flying job and took up blackjack instead. This covers most things from beginner to advanced, with true stories thrown into the mix. One of the great blackjack characters, US Book

g106, Winning Casino Blackjack for the Non-Counter, Avery Cardoza, £9.95pb, 136pp, Covers strategies for single and multiple decks, easy to understand charts, money management, and the Cardoza non-counters strategy, US Book

g130, Blackjack Your Way To Riches, Edward Canfield, £12.95pb, 207pp, Five experts pool their experience for this book. Learn money management, preserving and building your capital, tipping, fluctuation, junkets, taxes and much more, US Book g444, **Progression Blackjack**, Donald Dahl, £12.95pb, 153pp, Offers an alternative to counting cards. The system outlined here teaches how to make more money on the winning hands and lose less on the bad ones, suggesting card counting is out of date, US Book

g446, **Blackjack Essays**, Mason Malmuth, £19.95pb, 224pp, For advanced players, this covers card domination, theoretical concepts, blackjack biases, obsolete techniques, front loading, supplemental strategies and more, US Book

g464, **Blackbelt In Blackjack**, Arnold Snyder, £19.95pb, 181pp, For advanced players. Concerns two primary methods of attack - shuffle tracking and teaming - card counting strategies that are nearly impossible for casinos to detect, US Book

g493, **Theory of Blackjack**, Peter Griffin, £11.95pb, 262pp, One of the most important books on blackjack with charts, tables and formulas for almost every variation. For serious players, US Book

g577, **Basics Of Winning Blackjack**, J Edward Allen, £3.95pb, 58pp, Handy, easy to understand guide showing everything you need to know to play and win money at blackjack, US Book

g579, **Blackjack Secrets**, Stanford Wong, £14.95pb, 256pp, Both an introduction to counting and an explanation of how to apply winning techniques in casino's, US Book

g581, **Julians No Nonsense Guide to Blackjack**, John Julian, £16.95pb, 121pp, This includes the Sprint Strategies for exploiting multiple decks, single deck scan Techniques, basic strategy and card counting techniques and more, US Book

g582, **Winning Blackjack for Serious Players**, Edward Silberstang, £9.95pb, 183pp, Has chapters on card counting, single and multiple deck true count strategy, managing the dealer, money management self-discipline, and taking control of your game, US Book

g583, **Basic Blackjack**, Stanford Wong, £14.95pb, 224pp, May well be the most comprehensive discussion of basic strategy. Includes advice for proper play for almost any rule variation. All of Wong's books are nicely presented, US Book

g593, **Blackjack For Blood**, Bryce Carlson, £19.95pb, 250pp, Published in 92 and one of the bestsellers since. Well organised with simple, clear explanations; every serious player should have one., US Book

g748, **Beat The 6 Deck Game**, Arnold Snyder, £9.95pb, 64pp, A guidebook for serious players, US Book g749, **Professional Black**jack, Stanford Wong, £19.95pb, 352pp, The best overall card-counting syllabus on the market. Thorough, accurate, easy to understand, it is the ideal players manual. High Stakes Recommended title, US Book

g750, **Cheating at Blackjack** , Dustin Marks, £19.95pb, 225pp, Exceptional and controversial, the author had to write this one under an alias. If you get caught, we don't know you, if you don't get caught and win we do, US Book

g781, **Ultimate Blackjack Book**, Edward Early, £11.95pb, 149pp, Subtitled 'Playing Blackjack With Multiple Decks.' Has many charts and tables, and is for the intermediate to advanced player, US Book

g799, **Two Books on Blackjack**, Ken Uston, £4.95pb, 198pp, The first book is One Third Of A Shoe, telling how Uston and his team won $145,000 in 9 days in '79. The second is an instruction book on how to win in Atlantic City and Nevada, US Book

g877, **John Patrick's Advanced Blackjack**, John Patrick, £19.95pb, 319pp, For seasoned players who know the game but still manage to lose. Look out for trends and learn to count aces and faces, US Book

g909, **Best Blackjack**, Frank Scoblete, £14.95pb, 275pp, Includes: Strategies for single and multiple deck games, easy to master card-counting techniques, and how to take advantage of sloppy dealers! Beginners to advanced, US Book

g939, **Ultimate Blackjack Book**, Walter Thomason, £14.95pb, 128pp, Concentrates on multiple-deck play, with emphasis on card evaluation and card counting. Something for all levels here, US Book

g984, **Las Vegas Blackjack Diary**, Stuart Perry, £19.95pb, 212pp, The author documents 8 weeks of his playing in Nevada casino's. Contains his wins, losses, comments, and advice, and his reactions to being cheated, US Book

g1007, **Blackjack For The Clueless**, Walter Thomason, £12pb, 153pp, For beginners and occasional players, this offers solid strategies and advice to improve your game, US Book

g1065, **Blackjack Attack - Paying the Pro's Way**, Don Schlesinger, £19.95pb, 345pp, Expanded and enhanced edition of the classic blackjack book for advanced players, playing the pros' way, written by one of the most knowledgeable players in the world Recommended, US Book

g1079, **Complete Book of Blackjack**, £13.95pb, 204pp, For beginner to expert, takes you through basic strategy to counting to tournament-level.

Reynolds is a former dealer and has been playing for over 25 years, US Book

g1086, **Blackjack Wisdom**, Arnold Synder, £19.95pb, 203pp. A collection of writings by "the Bishop" culled from his many contributions to magazines over the years, UK Book

g1088, **Beat The 1 Deck Game**, Arnold Synder, £9.95pb, 64pp, A guidebook for the serious player, US Book

g1089, **Beat The 2 Deck Game**, Arnold Snyder, £9.95pb, 64pp, A guidebook for the serious player, US Book

g1095, **Beat The 8 Deck Game**, Arnold Snyder, £9.95pb, 64pp, Go on guess the blurb on this one. A guidebook for serious players, US Book

g1096, **Beat The 4 Deck Game**, Arnold Snyder, £9.95pb, 64pp, A guidebook for serious players who are attempting to get an edge over casinos, US Book

g1166, **Blackjack Bluebook**, Fred Renzey, £14pb, 188pp, Includes basics, and BJ Myths, Proper BJ Strategy, Borderline Hands, and the Key Card Count. Includes authors 'Mentor Count'., US Book

g1167, **Blackjack Reality**, David Morse, £34.95pb, 112pp, For astute beginners and experienced players. Morse takes you through card counting, signature cards, shuffle tracking, the Griffin order and money management, US Book

g1168, **Blackjack Magic**, Richard Sievers, £22.5pb, 129pp, The author believes progressive betting combined with his Sievers Strategy is the only way to win big at BJ, US Book

g1186, **Knock-out Blackjack**, Olaf Vancura, £17.95pb, 179pp, This has the K-O card counting system which is meant to be one of the easiest to learn. When you've done that you can progress to the 'K-O Preferred' system which is more complex, US Book

g1189, **Sklansky Talks Blackjack**, David Sklansky, £19.95pb, 140pp, Sklansky does away with all the Usual BJ charts and tables and 'talks' you through everything you need to know to beat the game, US Book

g1190, **Casino Blackjack**, Ron Modica, £12.95pb, 73pp, Includes Basic Strategy, Game Plan, Bankroll, Time, Streaks, Emotions, and Proper Play. Has charts for one to four decks but nothing on counting, US Book

g1263, **A Woman's Guide To Blackjack**, Angie Marshall, £9.99pb, 130pp, Covers the basics and card counting, and some of the other ways you can get one over the chauvinistic casino personnel, US Book g1276, **Blackjack The Smart Way - The Millennium Edition**, Richard Harvey, £19.95pb, 277pp, Author claims that he has discovered his own method for attacking casinos, a method that is more suited to the average everyday player, US Book

g1277, **Han's Blackjack Strategy**, Dr Sam Han, £19.95pb, 111pp, Subtitled, The simplest and the strongest Card Counting System, the author has his own simplified system claiming most others are far too complicated, US Book

g1297, **Blackjack Autumn**, Barry Meadow, £25pb, 255pp, Meadow packed his belongings into his car and went to play BJ in every Nevada casino. Well written, entertaining, and insightful. An original BJ book. Recommended title, US Book

g1323, **Cheating At Blackjack Squared**, Dustin Marks, £19.95pb, 202pp, This book represents the definitive resource on how professional con men cheat at Blackjack and other card games. The author, a former high-stakes cheater, explains an amazing array of specific moves with clear, understandable text and detailed,easy to understand illustrations, UK Book

g1373, **Twenty-First Century Blackjack**, Walter Thomason, £12.95pb, 186pp, Offers a revolutionary but practical alternative to card counting: a remarkable betting system that is easy to learn, simple to apply, impervious to casino harassment and most importantly, more profitable than flat or so-called inspired betting. As evidence, he offers a detailed analysis of thousands of hands of manually dealt play and hundreds of thousands of computer-simulated play. Using a totally unique approach, he compares the win/loss results of three different types of players (a card counter, a flat bettor, and a progressive bettor) who all played the same hands against the same dealer at the same time. Thomason even conducts live casino field tests, joined by several gaming experts who are pre-disposed to be sceptical of his system. The results of Thomason's unique comparative analysis will surprise you, and may very well shake the foundations of traditional blackjack theory (uumm). Although the book addresses some of the technical aspects of the game, no complicated math or statistical analysis is Used. This easy-to-read book is designed to help the average player improve his chances of winning more money, but it may also teach a thing or two to the expert player, US Book

g1433, **Blackjack Strategy: Tips and Techniques for Beating the Odds**, Michael Benson , £14.95pb, 176pp, Easy-to-understand guide to blackjack's basic strategy and card counting., US Book

g1494, **Chances are...: Your Winning Blackjack Strategy**, Matt Summers, £14.95pb, 144pp, This handbook presents a simple, intelligent strategy for maximising your chances of winning at blackjack. The author explains what the winning odds are for every combination of cards. He demonstrates how to size up the situation, calculate the odds and make the right decision, UK Book

g1531, **Blackjack for Winners**, Scott Frank, £11.95pb, 136pp, Scott Frank's new CORE system renders other blackjack strategies obsolete. Based on the principle that each deck can fluctuate between having a heavy or light Core that can predictably alter the nature of the game, players are taught to recognize to what degree the game is under their control. The techniques in this book are mathematically proven and thoroughly researched. A series of simple lessons leads readers step-by-step through every possible situation they might encounter at the table. In addition, popular card-playing myths are debunked, betting and tracking methods are discussed, and ways to cope with casino defensive tactics are provided, US Book

g1558, **Get the Edge at Blackjack**, John May, £13.95pb, 167pp, Some of the advantage-play techniques you'll learn from John May, one of the world's greatest advantage players: Hole Card Play, Glim Play, Optimal Betting, Card Steering, Card Sequencing, Card counting at Multiple Deck, Card Counting at single Deck, Shadow Play, Stacker Play, How to Use Progressions that Work, How to Beat the Preferential Shuffle, How to Beat Card Readers, How to Beat the Shuffle Machines and How to Beat Internet Casinos, US Book

g1566, **Blackjack's Hidden Secrets**, £11.95pb, Win without counting, US Book

g1576, **Blackjack, Blackjack, Blackjack**, Robert J. Neuzil, £9.95sp, 83pp, A system aimed at those casual players - a couple of weekends a year. You will learn how to properly play each and every hand, and how to manage your money for maximum return with minimum risk, US Book

g1581, **Power Blackjack: An Instructional Guide for the Serious Player**, Bryan Thibodeaux, £10sp, 110pp, Six sections including determining an individual's level of play, selecting the right strategy, its limitations and applications, how to scout casinos, keeping a journal, how to identify casino and player advantages, bet size and control of sessions, money management, direct betting and parlaying, selection and evaluation of popular systems, US Book

g1585, **Hit and Run: How to Beat Blackjack as a Way of Life**, Arnold Bruce Levy, £14.95pb, 166pp, If you frequent casinos, and blackjack is your game, Hit and Run is a must-read. If blackjack isn't your game, the strategies contained in this volume are sure to change your mind. With reproductions of actual scorecards, Levy demonstrates how you can systematically hit one casino after another and come home a victor almost every time. He also provides you scorecards demonstrating common errors, and explains them so you do not repeat his mistakes, US Book

14

g1598, **Blackjack 35 Tips to Make You a Winner!!** - A Basic Guide for the Game of 21, Walter Thomason, £5pb, 15pp, Does exactly what is says on the book, US Book

g1603, **Book of British Blackjack**, Dr Moshen Zadehkoochak, £11.99pb, 57pp, The result of several years of theoretical and practical research into the game of blackjack, as played in British casinos, is condensed into a very readable and informative book which will guide the reader, step by step, from the basics of the game to topics suitable to the more advanced player. The Book of British Blackjack covers: The rules of the game, The best playing strategy, Card counting methods and how they compare, Betting strategy and money management, Advanced method of strategy changes for extra gain, UK Book

g1625, **Blackjack: Take the Money and Run**, Henry J. Tamburin, £11.95pb, 148pp, Are You Serious About Winning? Well Are You? Blackjack: Take The Money And Run will teach you how to consistently walk away from the table with profits. The winning techniques are based on Dr. Tamburin's 25 years of experience as a winning blackjack player. You will learn, which games offer the most profit potential, a non-counting, winning strategy you can use even if you are a novice player, a unique streak count betting methodology for the intermediate player, a powerful advanced level system that will give you up to a 1.5% edge over the casinos, the risks involved in playing blackjack, how to play without fear of being barred, and last, but not least, the discipline to Take The Money and Run!, US Book

g1646, **Blackjack and the Law**, I Nelson Rose and Robert A Loeb, £24.95pb, 245pp, Two prominent attorneys in the field of gaming law look at the issues from the blackjacks' perspective, US Book

FINANCIAL BETTING

g1336, **Motley Fool UK Investment Guide**, David Berger, £12.99pb, pp, Shows readers why they need to invest; the power of compound interest; how to beat 90% of financial advisors at their own game; and why they need to be online and how to get there. The 2nd edition has been updated with revised listings of Websites and a new look, UK Book

g1337, **Motley Fool UK Investment Workbook**, Berger & Jackson, £9.99pb, 226pp, Companion to the other Motley Fool Guide: how to sort out personal finances, decide on investment objectives, choose companies to invest in, interpret numbers in a company report, UK Book

g1354, **Electronic Day Trading 101**, Sunny J.Harris, £19.5pb, 350pp, A top trading guru tells you everything you need to know about getting started as an online day trader, US Book

g1355, **Electronic Day Trader**, Friedfertig & West, £32.99hb, 208pp, Successful strategies for on-line trading, US Book

g1356, **Electronic Day Traders' Secrets**, Friedfertig & West, £19.99pb, 250pp, Learn from the best of the best day traders, US Book

g1390, **Online Investing: How to Find the Right Stocks at the Right Time**, Jon D. Markham, £16.99pb, 335pp, US Book

g1393, **UK Guide to Online Investing**, Michael Scott, £19.99pb, 234pp, This leads you to the best UK financial web sites. It tells you where to find free information relating to UK equity-based investments including shares, unit trusts, investment trusts and warrants, UK Book

g1413, **Investing Online for Dummies**, Kathleen Sindell , £23.99pb, 322pp, The fun and easy way to play the stock market - online. Your First Aid in finding hot investments on the web. Online trading and portfolio management - explained in plain English, US Book

g1418, **Sams Teach Yourself Today: e-Trading**: Researching & trading stocks, bonds & mutual funds online, Ray Tiernan, £12.99pb, 404pp, Guide to e-trading teaches how to get the most service for the least money by comparing features of various online trading firms, US Book

g1421, **Online Broker and Trading Directory,** Larry Chambers with Keith Johnson , £19.95pb, 250pp, Over 100 of the top online broker. Your guide to low-cost commissions and speedy executions. Lists the best features of each site, US Book

g1422, **Complete Idiot's Guide to Online Investing** - Second Edition, Doug Gerlach , Doug Gerlach , £17.50pb, 388pp, The quick and easy way to perfect your personal investment strategy using the Internet, US Book

GENERAL

g8, **Easy Money: Inside The Gamblers Mind**, David Spanier, £6.99pb, 233pp, An insiders analysis of the thrills, action, and intense emotional involvement that makes up the world of gambling, US Book

g14, **How To Win,** Mike Goodman, £6.99pb, 302pp, Gives solid advice on how you can become a tough player and tilt the odds. Covers horse racing, dice, slots, roulette, blackjack and poker., US Book

g53, **Theory of Gambling and Statistical Logic**, Richard Epstein, £29.95pb, 450pp, On gambling and its mathematical analysis. Covers the full range of games from penny matching, to Blackjack, other casino games and the stock market. Very technical, US Book

g56, **Casino Gambling**, Jerry L Patterson, £9.95pb, 236pp, Winning techniques for craps, roulette, baccarat, and blackjack, US Book

g59, **Darwin Ortiz: Casino Gambling**, Darwin Ortiz, £12.95pb, 268pp, The complete guide to playing and winning covering all the Usual casino games, US Book

g60, **Gambling Scams**, Darwin Ortiz, £10.99pb, 262pp, How scams work, how to detect them, how to protect yourself. Written by America's leading authority on crooked gambling, this is packed with good stuff, US Book

g67, **Caro On Gambling**, Mike Caro, £6.95pb, 177pp, This one covers Basic Truths, The Computer Age, Tactics and Advice, The Magic of Probability, Poker, and other thoughts. US Book

g107, **Casino Craps For The Winner**, Avery Cardoza, £7.95pb, 120pp, The prolific Cardoza with another good book for beginners to intermediates, US Book

g125, **Golf Gambling And Gamesmanship**, Gary Moore, £7.95pb, 150pp, The various chapters in this cover: handicapping, mental exercises, physical exercises, creative betting, and the 19th hole, US Book

g156, **How To Win At Craps**, Frank Hanback, £4.95pb, 190pp, For occasional players or seasoned gamblers, this is the complete crap shooters manual, US Book

g202, **Card Sharpers**, Robert Houdin, £5.95pb, 158pp, Translated from French, first published in 1860's, this has many card tricks exposed with a few basic diagrams, US Book

g207, **Crooks, Conmen & Cheats**, Eugene Villiod, £4.95pb, 131pp, First published in 1922, this is written by the famous French Detective. Includes burglars, pickpockets, confidence men and tricksters and much more., US Book

g224, **Expert At The Card Table**, S.W.Erdnase, £7.95pb, 218pp, First published in 1902, this was sold by magic supply stores as a work on magic. A complete course in card cheating and something of a classic, US Book

g229, **Gamblers Of Yesteryear**, Russell Barnhart, £9.95pb, 239pp, First published in 1983, this is an historical look at old time gangsters through the centuries, US Book

g235, **Handbook On Percentages**, C Shampaign, £4.95pb, 64pp, Written in the 1920's, this is an historical classic, showing how things were done in the prohibition era, US Book

g251, **Pari-Mutuel Betting**, James Hillis, £4.95pb, 69pp, Written mainly for horse players and first published in 1976, US Book

g260, **72 Hours At The Crap Table**, B Mickelson, £6.95pb, 62pp, This is just pages of actual dice rolls that you can test your system against, US Book

g261, **Sharps And Flats,** J N Maskelyne, £8.95pb, 335pp, The first definitive study on cheating, this became a classic when it was first published in 1894. Exposed, all you need to know to fleece the amateur gambler!, (as if you would!) US Book

g329, **How To Win At Gambling**, Avery Cardoza, £12.95pb, 312pp, This covers the usual casino stuff and also horse racing and bingo, US Book

g341, **Rich Uncle From Fiji,** M P Adams, £2.95pb, 64pp, A classic from 1911 containing numerous swindles for those who desire to take down and rope the public, US Book

g342, **The Right Way To Do Wrong**, Harry Houdini, £4.95pb, 96pp, Written by the great man himself, his is an expose of criminals and the ways they might trick you. First came out in 1906. US Book

g347, **Principles And Deceptions**, Arthur Buckley, £7.95pb, 221pp, Mainly concerns magic with coins, cards, and billiard balls. Written in 1948, US Book

g348, **Think And Grow Rich**, Napoleon Hill, £5.99pb, 254pp, This contains money making secrets that can change your life. Inspired by Andrew Carnegie's books, this is all about positive thinking and mental power, US Book

g351, **John Patricks Craps**, John Patrick, £18.95pb, 336pp, Includes an introduction to the game, plus a dozen systems including the Simple Hedge, Double and Extended Hedges Field Place, Six and Eight and Come, US Book

g360, **The Gambler**, Dostoevsky.F, £5.99pb, 238pp, Two extra novellas in this one as well: Bobok and A Nasty Story. One of the great Russian writers, The Gambler centres on Roulette, UK Book

g387, **How To Play Cribbage Well**, Frank Brown, £8.95pb, 61pp, Mostly on two handed crib but also has chapters on four handed and three to eight players. Also includes official rules., US Book

g398, **Life Management**, Lenart Meynert, £10pb, 186pp, Demonstrates that the best motivation for improving planning and goal orientation is laziness and a strong need for freedom. Avoid unnecessary work, stress, conflicts, and mistakes. (In English), UK Book

g411, **Scarne On Cards**, John Scarne, £5.99pb, 427pp, One of the classic card writers. Complete rules, how to spot cheaters, how to win at poker, gin, pinochle, blackjack, and lots of other games, US Book

g413, **Reference Guide To Casino Gambling**, Henry Tamburin, £6.95pb, 118pp, Basic rules and winning techniques for all the major casino games, US Book

g418, **Gin Rummy: How To Play & Win**, Sam Fry, £2.95pb, 57pp, 20 chapters for beginners to intermediates, US Book

g440, **Win At Cribbage**, Joe Wergin, £6.99pb, 170pp, Has chapters on Fundamentals, The Play, The Showing, Elementary Strategy, Five-Card, Variations, and Cribbing Along With The Masters, Reprinting at present. US Book

g447, **Getting The Best Of It**, David Sklansky, £29.95pb, 310pp, Divided into 6 sections: Mathematics of Gambling, General Gambling Concepts, Sports and Horse Betting, Poker, Blackjack, and Other Games, US Book

g448, **Gambling Theory**, Mason Malmuth, £29.95pb, 309pp, Well known gambling writer introduces you to the dynamic concept of non-self-weighting strategies, plus risk and fluctuation discussions, US Book

g486, **Coups And Cons**, Graham Sharpe, £4.95pb, 126pp, Written by Media Relations manager for William Hill, this is some of the scams that Sharpe has come across in his time, UK Book

g500, **Extra Stuff:Gambling Ramblings**, Peter Griffin, £11.95pb, 170pp, Famous blackjack writer and player with a collection of his other writings, covering a wide range of ideas and concepts, US Book g511, **Lose Less Win More At Gambling**, Jack Lennon, £9.95pb, 204pp, Written by a bookmaker for 40 years, this looks at gambling generally and horseracing. Includes a whole chapter on the tic tac code. Very limited stock, UK Book

g520, **Winning Craps Serious Player**, J Edward Allen, £12.95pb, 182pp, Everything you need to know here for beginners up to experts, US Book

g523, **Guerrilla Gambling**, Frank Scoblete, £12.95pb, 332pp, Attractive looking book which offers tips on all the usual casino games plus the more obscure ones. Good title!, US Book

g528, **A Licence To Print Money** , Jamie Reid, £8.99pb, 285pp, A journey through the gambling and bookmaking world, touted as one of the best of recent years Recommended, UK Book

g627, **The Money-Spinners**, Jacques Black, £7.99pb, 194pp, The bestselling book from our first catalogue, this concentrates mainly on blackjack and roulette and some of the characters from the past. An excellent read. Buy it!, UK Book

g658, **Prisoner's Dilemma**, William Poundstone, £12.95pb, 278pp, A fascinating biography of John Von Neuman plus game theory, and the puzzle of the bomb. Confused? So am I!, US Book

g681, **Basics Of Winning Slots**, J Edward Allen, £3.95pb, 58pp, Small handbook for beginners covering basic strategies for winning at slots., US Book

g689, **Las Vegas Guide**, Kranmar & Cardoza, £13.95pb, 238pp, This is a Useful travel guide if you're planning to go to the great city, US Book

g751, **Beat The House**, Frederick Lembeck, £12.95pb, 172pp, 16 ways to win at casino games by Using stock market system of dollar cost averaging. Investor sells increasing amounts as stock rises and buys as stock falls, supposedly guaranteeing a profit no matter what, US Book

g782, **Winning At Casino Gambling**, Lyle Stuart, £17pb, 320pp, Updated version of his earlier book, this is recommended by Mario Puzo of all people, and Stuart has a healthy record of large winnings not to be ignored, US Book

g784, **According To Hoyle**, Richard Frey, £5.99pb, 285pp, Briefly covers just about every game you would ever want to play and lots you could probably do without. Something of a classic, US Book

g817, **Patricks Advanced Craps**, John Patrick, £18.95pb, 400pp, Advanced concepts, angles, plays for crapshooters who already know the basics but need help in money management and table discipline, US Book

g842, **Complete Guide Winning Keno**, David Cowles, £14.95pb, 267pp, Cowle's entertaining and informative style, complete with anecdotes and insider strategies, makes learning to win at keno a pleasure. 51 chapters take you up to expert level, US Book

g843, **Encyclopedia Games & Gambling**, Edwin Silberstang, £14.95pb, 552pp, A modern Hoyle for sophisticated gamblers, this covers the usual casino games plus chess, sports events, and even strip poker, US Book

g864, **Teach Yourself Successful Gambling**, Belinda Levez, £5.99pb, 180pp, General book for beginners which covers racing, sports, casino games, lotteries, bingo, pools, and slots, UK Book

g878, **How Con Games Work**, M Allen Henderson, £9.95pb, 228pp, An entertaining read that tells you all you need to know about con men and their tricks. Learn the three-card monte, the badger game, pigeon drop, handkerchief switch, and many more, US Book

g879, **Gems Of Mental Magic**, Arthur Buckley, £4.95pb, 132pp, Written in 1947 this includes things like Astral Addition, Psychometry, Astrological Mentalism, Date Divination, Birthday Telepathy and much more, US Book

g898, **Basics Of Winning Craps**, J Edward Allen, £3.95pb, 59pp, Basic handbook giving a general overview of craps, and how to win. For beginners, US Book

g900, **Idiots Guide To Gambling Like A Pro**, Spector & Wong, £16.95pb, 320pp, I like these 'Idiots Guides', well laid out, easy to read, and full of Useful info'. This covers casino games and horses and sports betting, US Book

g970, **Zen and The Art Of Casino Gaming**, Miro Stabinsky, £18.95pb, 278pp, This takes a different angle from the Usual casino books, concentrating on maintaining the proper psychological and emotional balance needed to be a winner, US Book

g973, **Gin Rummy: How To Play And Win**, George Fraed, £9.95pb, 188pp, Includes: conventional gin, partnership gin, tournament gin, recognizing a cheater, early, middle and late strategy, and great gin tales and stories, US Book

g974, **Experts Guide To Casino Games**, Walter Thomason, £16.95pb, 249pp, A select group of pro' gamblers, each a winner at their particular game, offer advice to help you lose that sinking feeling, US Book

g1000, **Elliotts Golf Form 1999**, Keith Elliott, £20pb, 596pp, Full of statistics and records, the ultimate book for betting on golf. Foreword by Jimmy Tarbuck! We have extra copies of the 1997 edition, yours for only £4!, Latest edition also available. UK Book

g1005, **Secrets Of Winning Slots**, Avery Cardoza, £9.95pb, 175pp, Learn about single and multiple coin slots, multipliers, multi-payline and mega paylines, Big Bertha's, buy-your-play, mega progressives, and wild symbol machines, US Book

g1008, **Craps For The Clueless**, John Patrick, £12pb, 138pp, For beginners to advanced: initial buy-in to a detailed explanation of the odds, when to follow trends, money management, discipline etc , US Book

g1078, **Casino Gambling For Clueless**, Darwin Ortiz, £12.99pb, 268pp, A one volume course in casino education, this can turn you into a seasoned and knowledgable player. Craps, blackjack, keno, roulette, baccarat, and a lot more, US Book

g1082, **Twelve Grand**, Jonathan Rendall, £7pb, 250pp, Author was given £12,000 by his publisher but had to spend it all on gambling and then write a book about it. Sounds like a good idea but did it work? Recommended, UK Book

g1083, **Pari-Mutuel Betting**, Dan Coleman, £10pb, 52pp, This manual teaches how to determine the most effective types of betting tickets to purchase, and how to determine the optimum amounts to bet on each acceptable betting proposition, US Book

g1100, **Casino Answer Book**, John Grochowski, £12.95pb, 237pp, How to overcome the house advantage when you play blackjack, video poker, and roulette. US Book

g1126, **Complete Guide Memory Mastery**, Harry Lorayne, £7.99pb, 376pp, Lorayne's unique system of memory builders and his secrets for unlocking your memory power. This includes 2 other books of his: How to Develop A Super Power Memory, and Secrets Of Mind Power, US Book

g1147, **Rip-Offs, Cons And Swindles**, M.Allen Henderson, £9.95pb, 165pp, Covers such subjects as plastic crime, charity, investment and insurance fraud, and lots more, US Book

g1149, **Methods Of Disguise**, John Sample, £17.95pb, 258pp, Everything you need to know, whether you're an actor, a gambler, or an undercover cop. Over 130 pictures and easy to follow guidelines., US Book

g1152, **Disguise Techniques**, Edmond A.Macinaugh, £5.95pb, 82pp, The art of disguise, properly practised, requires mental conditioning, self-knowledge, and the ability to size up others and predict their movements. This tells you how, US Book g1153, **You Can't Cheat An Honest Man**, James Walsh, £19.95pb, 340pp, This is about Ponzi schemes, pyramid sales operations, and multilevel marketing, how they work, and why they're more common than ever, US Book

g1159, **Teach Yourself: Casino Games**. Belinda Levez, £3.99pb, 84pp, A short course for beginners. Covers poker, roulette, blackjack, punto banco, craps, and two up, US Book

g1160, **Teach Yourself: Card Games**, Belinda Levez, £3.99pb, 70pp, Basic handbook for beginners. Covers blackjack, baccarat, and lots of poker games, US Book

g1161, **The Hustler**, Walter Tevis, £6.99pb, 207pp, The Paul Newman film was based on this, a great novel by a great writer. We also stock his novel about chess 'The Queens Gambit's at 4.99. Also highly recommended, UK Book

g1162, **Oxford Dictionary Of Card Games**, David Parlett, £6.99pb, 360pp, Covers all the classic games, plus family and party games, patience and tarot, and some unusual ones too, UK Book

g1163, **Card Games.Pocket Reference**, Collins, £4.99pb, 314pp, Over 60 games are in this one, clearly laid out and illustrated. Four sections: family games, patience, children's games, and competitive games, UK Book

g1182, **Expert Strategy For Let It Ride**, Lenny Frome, £4.95pb, 10pp, Frome developed the odds table for this Shuffle Master game in 1992. Includes strategies for the video versions and the Colorado game. Crammed with critical data on hit frequency and distribution, US Book

g1204, **Lady Luck**, Warren Weaver, £8.95pb, 392pp, First published in 1963, this has chapters on mathematical probability and expectation, the law of averages, binomial experiments, probability and gambling, US Book

g1206, **Mathematics Of Games & Gambling**, Edward Packel, £20pb, 140pp, Introduces and develops some of the important and elementary maths needed for rational analysis of various gambling and game activitie., US Book

g1221, **The Which Guide To Gambling**, Lowe And Clark, £9.99pb, 278pp, Excellent book giving a general overview of gambling in this country. Three sections covering: what is gambling all about, investment gambles, and pure gambles, UK Book

g1226, **Taking Chances**, John Haigh, £19pb, 326pp, Winning with probability. Analyses a wide range of situations in which chance plays a role, such as the lottery, football pools, roulette, and card games, UK Book

g1233, **Gambling Card Sharps**, Scott E. Lane, £19.95pb, 220pp, Packed with info about how to recognise card cheaters, well illustrated showing methods and techniques. For expert card sharps, US Book

g1234, **The Man With The $100, 000 Breasts**, Michael Konik, £24.95hb, 234pp, Entertaining book about some of the more bizarre bets undertaken in the US. Even has a picture of the man in the title story!, US Book

g1235, **14 Million To One,** Graham Sharpe, £8.99pb, 160pp, The ever popular Sharpe with another book listing bizarre real-life bets, UK Book

g1238, **Abracadabra**, Nat Schiffman, £25pb, 440pp, This is an insiders look at what goes on at a magic show, behind the scenes, and in the mind of the magician, US Book

g1240, **Fools Die**, Mario Puzo, £6.99pb, 530pp, US novel by the author of The Godfather, about luxurious casinos, high rollers, hustlers, manipulators and hookers, US Book

g1241, **The Dice Man**, Luke Rhinehart, £6.99pb, 540pp, Controversial, outrageous, bestseller from 1971 about a man whose every decision in life is governed by a throw of the dice. This leads him into very murky waters indeed!, US Book

g1242, **Scarne's Encylopedia Of Card Games**, John Scarne, £16pb, 400pp, A classic in its field, here is all you ever wanted to know about the histories and variations of the worlds most popular card games. Indispensible, US Book

g1245, **Playing For Profit,** Peter Walker, £4.99pb, 93pp, UK book which is a guide to profitable betting on the lottery, pools, and horse racing, UK Book

g1246, **Complete Book Of Golf Games**, Scott Johnston, £9.95pb, 96pp, Features over 80 great game and tournament formats, illustrated with cartoons. Numerous quotes from famous and anonymous golf lovers., US Book

g1247, **40 Years A Gambler On Mississippi**, George H.Devol, £12.95pb, 300pp, Reprint of 1887 classic, and a very sought after title about a notorious riverboat gambler and cheat. He cheated at poker, faro, monte, and any other game that was going, US Book

g1248, **A Gamblers Bedside Reader**, John Gollehon, £15.99pb, 176pp, 46 gambling tales intended to entertain, educate and inspire. They are all true, and while some are amusing, others are almost unbelievable, US Book

g1261, **The Big Con**, David W.Maurer, £14.99pb, 280pp, A classic first published in 1940, this is a collection of true stories about grifters and con men, US Book

g1262, **Casino Gambling The Smart Way**, Andrew Glazer, £12.99pb, 254pp, Rather than concentrating on specific games this has sections on Gambling Systems, Know Thyself, A Winning Frame Of Mind, and looks at slots and lotteries, US Book

g1269, **Keno Runner**, David Kranes, £10pb, 276pp, A weird, surreal but virtually unknown novel about the Vegas experience. David Spanier's favourite gambling novel, US Book

g1271, **The Crossroader,** Moore & Darring, £8.95pb, 177pp, Memoirs of a professional gambler called Junior Moore, US Book

g1275, **The Addictive Personality**, Craig Nakken, £11.95pb, 129pp, First published in '88, this discusses gambling as an addiction, but also covers all forms of addiction as well, US Book

g1290, **Number**, John McLeish, £20pb, 266pp, The history of numbers and how they shape our lives. A fascinating journey through time and space tracing the immense variety of mathematical concepts through world history, US Book

g1291, **Frauds, Ripoffs And Con Games**, Victor Santoro, £14.95pb, 200pp, Examines short cons, gypsy cons, white collar criminals, and how they operate. Also credit card scams, telemarketing scams, securities swindles etc, US Book

g1293, **Why Do Buses Come In Threes?**, Eastaway & Wyndham, £20pb, 156pp, An entertaining look at how maths and the laws of probability are constantly at work in our lives, affecting everything we do from getting a date to catching a bus, US Book

g1298, **Telling Lies**, Paul Ekman, £14.95pb, 366pp, Discusses poker faces and attempting to conceal emotion in poker. Also at detecting deceit from words, voice, body, facial clues, the polygraph etc., US Book

g1301, **Probability: An Introduction**, Samuel Goldberg, £10.95pb, 322pp, From 1960, this covers Probability in Finite Sample Spaces, sophisticated Counting, random Variables, and binomial Distribution, US Book

g1307, **The Players Men Who Made Vegas**, Jack Sheehan, £18.95pb, 224pp, Essays by different writers on the men behind the success of Vegas, such as Bugsy Siegel, Benny Binion, Howard Hughes, Cliff Jones, Moe Dalitz and more, US Book

g1313, **Betting To Win**, Luke Johnson, £7.99pb, 176pp, A general look at gambling in this country, this covers pools, lottery, bingo, horses, greyhounds, slots, psychology, cheats, and probability, UK Book

g1316, **Magic Tricks**, Card Shuffling, Etc, S.Brent Morris, £25pb, 148pp, The full title continues and Dynamic Computer Memories. Explores the interconnections between these, and the mathematics of card shuffling, US Book

g1327, **Big Julie Of Las Vegas**, Edward Linn, £14.95pb, 218pp, Classic from 1974 about Julius Weintraub who created junkets in the 60s and 70s. A colourful account of Vegas 20 years and the characters who inhabited it, US Book

g1328, **The Big Bankroll**, Leo Katcher, £14.95pb, 369pp, Reveals the life of a powerful American gambler, a man who transformed organised crime from a thuggish activity into a big business, run like a corporation, with himself at the top. This biography includes Arnold Rothstein's crimes, his luck, his murder and his missing millions, US Book

g1329, **Trader Vic**, Victor Sperandeo, £18.95pb, 304pp, This guide offers an investment approach built upon three principles: preservation of capital, consistent profits and the pursuit of superior returns. It then outlines specific proven strategies which any investor can apply. The book also explains the inter-relationships amongst the world and national economies, monetary and fiscal policies, and the business cycle. It shows how investors can use these insights in developing an investment strategy., US Book

g1330, **Dice Games Properly Explained**, Reiner Knizia, £3.99pb, 224pp, This book explains almost 150 games and variations, compiled by world authority Dr. Reiner Knizia. The collection ranges from early games whose origins are lost in the mists of antiquity, right up to newly invented games that have never been published before. The rules of all games are explained lucidly, and the tactical advice given is explicit, UK Book

g1338, **Play Winning Cribbage**, Delynn Colvert, £10.95pb, 154pp, A good guide for the fundamentals of the games as well as a thorough guide to help improve on the basics of the game, UK Book

g1339, **Cribbage A New Concept**, John E.Chambers, £6.95pb, 174pp, This begins with the basics, moves to discarding techniques; scoring points; the count; board strategy; offensive and defensive positions; Advanced Strategy Techniques including choosing your discard; (a mathematical approach) and the rules, US Book g1340, **The Dice Doctor**, Sam Grafstein, £19.95pb, 146pp, Revised and Expanded, US Book

g1357, **Hello Rebel**, F.J.Harper, £12.99pb, pp, This has systems and staking plans for dog racing, roulette, fixed odds football, horse racing, internet gambling and the lottery, UK Book

g1361, **Gambling, Collins Gem**, £4.99pb, 192pp, An introductory chapter explains what odds are for the layman and tells how to calculate your expected return. Chapters on horse racing, football pools, greyhound racing, sports betting, and casino games explain each type of bet and how to maximise your winnings. Games of skill are also covered in detail and further reading suggested for those who want to enter the big time in games such as Poker, Bridge and backgammon. The popular activities of those who don't regard themselves as gamblers are slot machines, bingo, lotteries and sweepstakes, but even here there is sound advice which the reader can follow, even if the opportunity to win in the long term is severely limited. Finally the human side of gambling such as cheats, hustlers and gambling addition will bring back to earth everyone who thinks betting has a sexy image, UK Book

g1371, **Super Casino: Inside the New Las Vegas**, Pete Earley, £25pb, 386pp, Pete Earley traces the evolution of Las Vegas - when moguls, mobsters, and the world's top entertainers came together to create this ultimate monument to American excess. This fascinating book reveals the real stories of well-known power brokers like Steve Wynn, Vegas legends like Howard Hughes and Bugsy Siegel, and the gripping rise and fall and rise again of the entreneurs behind one of the largest gaming corporations in the nation, the colossus Circus Circus, to which the author was given unique access., US Book

g1376, **The Predictors**: How a Band of Maverick Physicists Set Out to Beat Wall Street, Thomas A.Bass, £18.99pb, 309pp, Thomas Bass first made readers aware of cult heroes Farmer and Packard in The Newtonian Casino, in which he chronicled their assault on the casinos of Las Vegas. Here Bass takes US inside their start-up company, at first a group of long haired Ph.Ds with no furniture and no money, as they nervously test their computer forecasting models. As confidence builds, Farmer and Packard buy a company Italian suit and takes turns travelling in the centres of financial power, where they find investors. Yet the real test is still to come: what will happen when they go live with real money? A delight for anyone who has ever dreamed of finding that edge to beat the system, UK Book

g1377, **Liar's Poker**, Michael Lewis, £6.99pb, 298pp, Michael Lewis retired from being a bond salesman at the age of 28, having risen from being a mere trainee. He looks back at his career, at the Golden Age of banking, at the company he worked for and the memorable figures within it, and at the spectacle of the financial boom which marks the 80s, UK Book g1378, **Gambling on the Internet**, Geoff Mangum, £4.95pb, 155pp, This handy, pocket-sized guide will lead you to the very best gambling sites on the web - most of which are completely free. Full site addresses in a variety of categories are provided, with an impartial review of content, speed, layout and reliability, UK Book

g1380, **The Complete Idiot's Guide to Online Gambling**, Mark Balestra, £15.99pb, 320pp, Discover quick and easy ways to.. Find the exciting gambling spots online. Practice your wagering savvy at free games. Learn how to play all the Usual games, such as blackjack, craps, roulette, and many more. Get involved in online bingo tournaments, keno, and even lotteries. Visit all the hot sports wagering sites to check the odds, US Book

g1384, **The Search for the Dice Man**, Luke Rhinehart, £6.99pb, 381pp, You can let the dice decide ... but you can't choose your own father Larry Rhinehart is the son of an infamous father - the renegade psychiatrist Luke Rhinehart, otherwise known as the Dice Man. Luke became a cult in the seventies, inspiring thousands to follow him into the anarchic world of Dice Living, where every decision is made not by the self, but the roll of a dice. Larry is emphatically not a follower. He has grown up to have a great respect for order and control. A wealthy wall Street analyst, all set to marry the boss's daughter, Larry has got life where he wants it. Until rumours begin to circulate about the reappearance of his long-vanished father - and Larry's carefully organized world begins to look a lot less certain, US Book

g1397, **24/7: Living It Up and Doubling Down in the New Las Vegas**, Andres Martinez , £13.95pb, 329pp, In the spring of 1998, mild-mannered, Ivy League-educated Andres Martinez took $50, 000 - most of the advance his publisher was paying for this book - and headed to Las Vegas for 30 days, ten casinos, and a wild ride through the belly of a neon beast. The result: this brilliant, often hilarious chronicle of gambling in a city where everyone dreams of hitting the jackpot, US Book

g1398, **Deal Me In: 101 Columns the Casino Operators Don't Want You to Read**, Mark Pilarski , £14.95pb, 210pp, Interesting collection of gaming articles, US Book

g1410, **Taking Chances: Winning with probability**, John Haigh , £8.99pb, 330pp, Would you like to beat the bookies? Win at Monopoly? Or understand just how (unlikely) you are to win the lottery? The answers lie in probability theory, to which Taking Chances provides an entertaining and accessible guide. By describing and analysing a wide range of situations in which chance plays a role, such as the lottery, football pools, roulette, and card games, John Haigh guides the reader round many of the common pitfalls and controversies that surround probability, Recommended, UK Book

28

g1411, **Risky Business: America's Fascination with Gambling**, Ronald M.Pavalko , £45.95pb, 191pp, A current, objective look at the role gambling plays in our society and in our personal life, US Book

g1412, **Finding the Edge: Mathematical Analysis of Casino Games**, ed Bill Eadington, £40pb, 441pp, Mathematical analysis of casino games, US Book

g1414, **Beat Web Casinos.Com,** Bill Haywood , £14.95pb, 198pp, This will show you how to; make money gambling in your living room, recognize fly-by-night scam operations, discern which major eCasinos are honest, Handle gaming software crashes, complain, and get paid!, US Book

g1415, **The Winners Guide to Casino Gambling**, Edwin Silberstang, £14.95pb, 469pp, Newly revised and expanded edition, more vital tactics, tips and professional secrets to give you an even sharper winning edge, US Book

g1417, **All In**, Mitchell Symons , £6.99pb, 344pp, Set in the twilight world of all-night poker games, betting shop coups and spread-betting mania. This debut novel is the darkly funny diary of one man dicing with death, Recommended, UK Book

g1437, **Betting on Rugby**, Michael Nevin , £10sp, 78pp, Complete articles from Odds On, March 1997 - July 2000, UK Book

g1440, **Literary Companion to Gambling**, Annabel David-Goff, £20hb, 246pp, An anthology of prose and poetry, UK Book

g1442, **Not Quite Cricket**, Pradeep Magazine, £5.99pb, 165pp, This intelligent study of the state of Indian cricket looks at the murkier side of a sport that has enveloped a whole nation. Behind the countenance of World Cup glory and titanic test series there lies a disturbing reality of corruption and criminality which is explored here through interview and research, UK Book

g1449, **Casino Gambling Behind the Tables**, John Alcamo, £7.99pb, 150pp, Jammed packed with inside information from casino managers, hosts and executives. Uncommon insights into the casino world to help you become a better player, US Book

g1450, **Scandals of '51,** Charley Rosen, £14.95pb, 263pp, How the gamblers almost killed college basketball, US Book

g1452, **Gambling Game and Psyche**, Bettina L Knapp, £19.95hb, 308pp, Attempt to answer the question of why have people from all backgrounds been drawn to gambling over the last thousand years, US Book g1453, **Introduction to Casino and Gaming Operations**, Denis P. Rudd and Lincoln H. Marshall, £61hb, 262pp, Helpful information on how the casino and gaming industry is run and how to use this information to build productive and successful careers, US Book

g1454, **Jim Feist's Sports Betting Guide 2000-2001**, Jim Feist, £6.5pb, 276pp, Experts show you how to win and where to bet: Football (American), Basketball, Baseball, Hockey, Horseracing, US Book

g1456, **Win 90% of your Golf Bets**!, Action Al Williams, £24.95hb, 198pp, Contains interesting insight into the great gamblers including Mysterious Montague, Titantic Thompson, Fat Man Stanovich, 3-Iron Gates and Bobby Riggs, US Book

g1462, **Nocturnal Creations**: The Impromptu Card Illusions of Paul Gordon, Paul Gordon , £25hb, 160pp, Nocturnal Creations is Paul Gordon's first hardback publication detailing his unique brand of impromptu Card Magic with a regular deck of cards. Each and every effect (in fact; 47 effects) has been Used by Paul Gordon in the professional field of entertainment. All 47 items are (were) designed for the working magician who has basic to semi-advanced skills. If you understand the basics of card magic, Nocturnal Creations will give you 47 miracles including the already classic, Gordon Diary Trick. This effect is possibly the only impromptu version of its genre and ilk. With this effect, a diary is shown to contain random playing cards on each of the 365(6) days of the year. The spectator names any date in the year and chooses a playing card from a borrowed deck. Amazingly, the entry in the diary is the same as the chosen card. The methodology doesn't employ any memorised deck system, stacked deck, duplicate diaries or sleight of hand. In other words, anybody can do it. This effect, and the 46 others are used by the world's top professionals. Nocturnal Creations contains 160 pages of exciting text, enhanced by 53 line illustrations to aid the teaching, UK Book

g1463, **Protean Card Magic**, Paul Gordon , £22pb, pp, Protean Card Magic is Paul Gordon's second hardback publication detailing his unique brand of impromptu Card Magic with a regular deck of cards. Each and every effect (in fact; 42 effects) has been Used by Paul Gordon in the professional field of entertainment. All 42 items are (were) designed for the working magician who has basic to semi-advanced skills. If you understand the basics of card magic, Protean Card Magic will give you 42 miracles. Protean Card Magic contains 145 pages of exciting text, enhanced by 57 line illustrations to aid the teaching, UK Book

g1465, **Cause and Effect**: Card Magic for the Millennium, Paul Gordon , £28pb, 225pp, Cause And Effect is Paul Gordon's third hardback publication detailing his unique brand of Card Magic with a regular deck of cards. Each and every effect (in fact; 66 effects) has been Used by Paul Gordon in the professional field of entertainment. All 66 items are (were) designed for the working magician who has basic to semi-advanced skills. If you understand the basics of card magic, Cause And Effect will give you 66 miracles including We Have Lift-Off; possibly one of the most incredible effects of the last decade, and what is more, it is one of the easiest! Cause And Effect contains a massive 225 pages of easy-to-read text, enhanced by 170 lucid line illustrations to aid the teaching, UK Book

g1467, **109 Ways to Beat the Casinos**, Walter Thomason, £13.95pb, 147pp, Six renowned casino experts have teamed up to provide you, the recreational gambler, with easy-to-understand advice that should improve your playing skills and help reduce the casino's built-in advantage over you, US Book

g1468, **Fell's Official Know-It-All Guide**: Casino gambling, Dennis Harrison, £16.95pb, 309pp, Featured are the major casino games, including, blackjack, poker, slot machines, roulette. craps. With special chapters on video poker, software and cyberspace, US Book

g1477, **Secrets of the New Casino Games**, Marten Jensen, £14.95pb, 144pp, You'll learn how to play and win at nine new casino games - Let It Ride, Caribbean Stud Poker, Three Card Poker, Pai Gow Poker, Spanish 21, Pai Gow, Sic Bo and War!, US Book

g1479, **Games, Gods and Gambling**: A History of Probability and Statistical Ideas, F. N David, £9.95pb, 275pp, This well-researched engaging history traces the roots of the science of probability and chance back to origins of counting , the decimal scale, and games played with dice. By charting the development of increasingly sophisticated techniques for gambling and games of chance, the author illustrates the birth of such concepts as combinatorial analysis, andomness, the calculus of probabilities, and the forerunners of modern statistics, US Book

g1498, **The Unofficial Guide to Casino Gambling**, Basil Nestor, £15.95pb, 400pp, Provides information on odds, good bets, and wagers one should never make, discusses insider secrets, provides money-saving techniques and time-saving tips, and includes checklists and charts., UK Book

g1513, **Play the Game:** A Compendium of Rules, Roger Proud and Darren Bellas, £7.99pb, 128pp, Volume One covers games which can be played in a casino and also games which can be played at home. Includes following games Roulette Backgammon Bridge Canasta Poker whist Chess Dominoes Dice, UK Book

g1519, **Don't Leave It to Chance** - A Guide for Families of Problem Gamblers, Edward J. Federman, £13.95pb, 224pp, Filled with useful information and practical advice based on the latest research and a sophisticated understanding of problem gambling, US Book

g1520, **Sex, Drugs, Gambling and Chocolate**, Dr A. Thomas Horvath,

£12.99pb, 224pp, There is an alternative to 12-step! Eliminate or reduce any type of addictive behaviour with this practical and effective workbook. treat addictions as a whole, rather than dealing separately with each issue (e.g. drinking, smoking, overeating, gambling...Dr. Horvath's rational approach is based on scientifically validated methods and emphasized taking responsibility for your actions, without requiring an allegiance to a higher power. Teaches readers about consequences (and even possible benefits) of addictive behaviour, alternative coping methods, choice, understanding and coping with urges, building a lifestyle, preventing relapse. Includes dozens of exercises, self-study, guidelines for individual change plans, UK Book

g1523, **Card Games for Dummies**, Barry Rigal, £15.99pb, 345pp, With this tome , you'll have all the information you need to play and win the most popular card games. Games featured include baccarat, Barbu, Blackjack, Bridge, Canasta, Clobyosh, Cribbage, Eights, Euchre, Fan Tan, Gin Rummy, Go Fish, Hearts, Oh Hell, Old Maid, Pinochle, Piquet, Rummy, Poker, President, Setback, Solitaire, Spades and Whist, US Book

g1524, **Statistics in Sport**, Jay Bennett (Editor), £65hb, 312pp, Sports data receive a lot of attention in the media, but disciplined analysis of the data is rarely covered. For decades, statistical researchers throughout the world have been published research on sports statistics, but this research has been spread thinly over many journals and conferences. This book is the first publication in over 20 years to provide a comprehensive survey of statistical applications in sports. Includes a chapter on predicting outcomes, UK Book

g1526, **Gambler's Guide to the World**: The Inside Scoop from a Professional Player on Finding the Action, Beating the Odds, and Living It Up Around the World, Jesse May, £16pb, 307pp, Jesse May, an intrepid gambler, experienced poker pro, and critically acclaimed writer, has travelled across America and around the world in search of the hottest gambling action. From sports betting in Costa Rica to high-stakes Vegas poker, from caviar and vodka in Moscow to funnel cakes and submarine sandwiches in Atlantic City, May has tried his hand and his luck at gambling and indulged in the good life across the globe. An insightful travel guide with a lively travel narrative to create a totally unique guidebook to the choicest sites in the world, US Book

g1527, **Gambling Times Guide to Winning Systems and Methods** - Volume Two, £5.95pb, 135pp, For the first time in the history of gambling, 12 complete strategies for casino gaming and sports wagering are yours in one single volume. These winning systems and methods have been created for the novice and the professional gambler and are guaranteed to give you a calculated opportunity to win every time you place your bet, US Book g1529, **Losing Your $hirt**, Mary Heineman, £14.95pb, 191pp, This book provides help for the marriage of compulsive gamblers. Ways to help end the compulsive gambling habit. Ways to help those affected by loved ones who gamble compulsively. Stories from compulsive gamblers and their families in recovery. Within these pages is a warm, non-threatening approach to the problem families encounter with compulsive gambling. Here you will find the support to recover from the reported experiences of many people who share the life of life disorder brings, US Book

g1530, **Card Games properly Explained**, Arnold Marks, £9.95pb, 220pp, Includes Whist, Solo, Clobbiosh, Contract Bridge, Belot, Piquet, Poker, Cassino, Black Maria, Kaluki, Canasta, Cribbage, Pontoon, Competitions, Five Hundred, Brag, Gin Rummy, Napoleon, Auction Bridge, UK Book

g1538, **Beyond Counting** - Exploiting Casino Games from Blackjack to Video Poker, James Grosjean, £39.95pb, 223pp, It is rare for a relatively unknown author to burst onto the scene with the brilliance that is shown in this first endeavour. This work shows that blackjack isn't the only game in town. He reveals legal way to beat three-card poker, craps, baccarat and the big six. This book is not for beginners or amateurs and these methods are not easy (but they're REAL). 56 chunky chapters with plenty of mathematical formulas to affirm the information, US Book

g1540, **Probability - Odds Line and Optimal Dutching Programs**, Michael J. Pascual, £20sp, 100pp, Provides a quick uncomplicated method for determining how much to wager on more than one horse in a rare (dutching) in order to maximise profit, US Book

g1541, **Gambling - Crime or Recreation**?, , £29pb, 162pp, Meant as a school study guide providing primary and secondary sources including graphs and tables. he series deals with contemporary issues or social problems, US Book

g1542, **Casino Comics**, Mark Lewis, £6.99pb, 188pp, A collection of cartoon with a gambling theme, some funny some not, you know how it is!, US Book

g1543, **Overcoming Compulsive Gambling** - A Self-Help Guide Using Cognitive Behavioural Techniques, Alex Blaszczynski, £7.99pb, 212pp, Explains how gambling problems can develop and who is at risk. Contains a complete self-help programme and monitoring sheets. Is based on clinically proven techniques of cognitive therapy, UK Book

g1560, **Elliotts Golf Form 2001**, Keith Elliott, £24pb, 732pp, The seventh volume of this superbly comprehensive annual of golf betting. Includes Elliott's eleven laws of golf betting, The Agony and Ecstasy, The DYM systems's record year, Mental skills in golf, Let's have prize money in £S not Euros, Is golf still an oasis in the desert of commercial sleaze?,

Golf Betting, Golf betting disputes, Golf Betting 2001, The European Tour Form 2000, The American Tour Form 2000, The World Golf Championship (WGC) Tournaments 2000, The Majors 2000, Presidents Cup 2000, Player Profiles, The European Tour Players, The American Tour Players, Statistical Appendices. Will always be recommended, UK Book

g1563, **RFO Guide Golf 2001**, £4.95pb, 240pp, Well produced and invaluable guide to the forthcoming Golf season, UK Book

g1571, **And Nothing But The Truth**?, Deon Gouws, £9.99pb, 213pp, One of the first of the expected avalanche of books involving Hansie and match fixing. Read how Kepler Wessels disputes some of Cronje's evidence brought before the King Commission. Professor Tim Noakes reflects on how the relationship between Cronje and the cricketing staff deteriorated. Craig Matthews admits to awareness of Cronje's obsession with money. Ray McCauley says (Hansie) certainly answered all questions truthfully, but I'm not sure that he's been asked everything, SA Book

g1577, **Basketball - Picking Winners Against the Spread**, A J Friedman, £7.95pb, 64pp, Well we try and be comprehensive! , US Book

g1578, **Thrifty Gambling**, John G Brokopp, £13.95pb, 153pp, Explains the best methods for recreational gamblers to use to reduce their risk while still giving them a good shot to win and a great deal of fun!, US Book

g1579, **Gambling: Crime or Recreation** (The Information Series on Current Topics), £29pb, 162pp, Primarily designed to be a resource for study including many primary and secondary sources. Topics include Gambling - An American Tradition, Gambling and the Government - Laws, Court Cases, Lobbying, and Politics, An Overview of Gambling, Pari-Mutuel Betting - Horses, Dogs and Jai Alai, Casino Gambling - Land-Based Casinos, Casino Gambling-On the Water, Casino Gambling-Native American Reservations, Lotteries-Legal and alluring, Bingo and Other Charitable Games, Illegal Gambling in America, Public Opinions About Gambling, US Book

g1587, **Gambling Expertise Through Basic Probability**, Bob Riley, £19.95sp, 92pp, Instruction through clear and concise methods highlighted by many examples illustrating every point, US Book

g1589, **Fistful of Kings**, John Brotherton, £29.95hb, 369pp, John Brotherton is an ex-Green Beret and high level casino executive. Embroiled in the Louisiana casino scandal that recently convicted ex-Louisiana Governor Edwin Edwards, Brotherton goes to Russia and runs a casino backed by TV and movie start Chuck Norris. Norris leaves Brotherton, his wife and two other Americans behind to face almost certain death at the hands of the Russian mob. He escapes Moscow with the help of US Senator John Breaux and a mysterious intelligence operative, Brotherton arrives back on US soil threatened because of what he knew and has spent the next two years in isolation writing Fistful Of King., US Book

g1590, **Gambling a Family Affair**, Angela Willens, £6.99pb, 123pp, This title, part of the Overcoming Common Problems series, offers advice to families and those who have a gambling problem. It includes case histories, and provides a list of helpful organizations, UK Book

g1591, **Winning Lottery Combinations** - Volume 1, Stephen B. Richter, £4.95pb, 64pp, This book will give you an easy way to select your own lottery numbers AND significantly increase your probability of winning prizes at every level, UK Book

g1595, **Scarne's New Complete Guide to Gambling**, , £20pb, 871pp, Every aspect of gambling at games of chance and skill is covered here: official rules; correct odds and house percentages; advice and instruction on playing strategy; explanations of swindling methods and how to detect them, US Book

g1600, **Waddingtons Illustrated Card Games**, , £9.99pb, 400pp, A veritable encyclopaedia of card games, amiliar and lesser-known, from all over the world. An essential reference book for every card-player, a treasure-trove for family evenings, UK Book

g1601, **Card Games**, Paul Barnett and Ron Tiner, £4.95hb, 96pp, Over twenty card games, ranging from the popular to the more unusual, are described with diagrams, colourful illustrations, and instructions. UK Book

g1602, **How to Win at Casino Gambling**, Roger Gros, £9.99pb, 160pp, Covering everything from the psychology of the casino layout to understanding the odds and placing the best bets. Games covered: Blackjack, Poker, Roulette, Baccarat, Craps, Slots, Video Poker plus the exotic casino games, UK Book

g1607, **World's Greatest Card Tricks**, Bob Longe, £3.99pb, 128pp, A compendium of card tricks to impress family and friends, this book supplies all the skills and techniques needed. Each trick is presented as though the author was actually performing it, complete with banter and conversation, US Book

g1608, **Mark Wilson's Little Book of Card Tricks**, Mark Wilson, £3.5hb, 128pp, Filled with easy to magic tricks presented in miniature book format, UK Book

g1613, **Beating the Casinos at their Own Game**, Peter Svoboda, £19.95pb, 278pp, Explains which games of chance offer the best and worst odds.Presents step-by-step instructions for playing the most popular casino games Analyses the most popular betting systems and explains why the majority don't work Includes original systems for winning at craps and roulette. Presents important money-management techniques, Explains the difference between house odds and your true odds Provides a basic understanding of probabilities and odds, US Book

g1617, **The Book of the Die:** A Handbook of Dice Living, Luke Rhinehart, £9.99pb, 313pp, A playful book of parables, essays, thoughts, ideas and practical instructions and reminiscences on dice-ing that is designed to be dipped into as an introduction to, or a companion to, the dice life, UK Book

g1618, **Running Scared** - The Life and Treacherous Times of Las Vegas Casino King, Steve Wynn, £15pb, 376pp, Describes the casino mogul's tremendous power in Nevada, and why a confidential Scotland Yard report deprived him of a license to open a casino in London. It offers an intimate look beyond the green felt tables and the feverish whirl of slot machines never before available. Recommended , US Book

g1620, **Budget Gambling,** John Gollehon, £14.99pb, 232pp, Play at low risk for high rewards including free game cards, US Book

g1621, **Lester Ben Benny Binion**, Mary Ellen Glass, £26pb, 95pp, Some Recollections of a Texas and Las Vegas Gaming Operator - An Oral History conducted by Mary Ellen Glass, US Book

g1622, **Yes, You Can Win!,** Bob Stupak, £5.95pb, 149pp, This is a fast-paced, easy-to-understand handbook that will improve your play in craps, roulette, 21 and other casino games, US Book

g1628, **Card Tricks**, Trevor Day, £7.99pb, 252pp, A compact and comprehensive guide to performing over 80 card tricks. Covers the basic skills nedded to perform the tricks, and advice on how to practise and develop a good performance. Includes step-by-step instructions and explanatory diagrams for all the tricks, UK Book

g1629, **Magic Tricks & Card Tricks**, Wilfrid Jonson, £5.95pb, 94pp, Teaches you to perform Card in the Pocket, Turn Over, Hypnotism, The 13 Principle, Eight Kings, and some 40 others, along with easy methods for false shuffling, palming, the glide, prepared cards, and many similar techniques, US Book

g1630, **Bankroll Contol**: The Mathematics of Money Management, M Pascual, £35sp, 118pp, Includes, money management for achieving maximum profit (single bet case), The Group Overlay a) Optimal Group Betting b) using the Computer Program, The simultaneous Two-Bet Case a)Two Bets on the Same Contestant b) Two Bets on Different Contestants, Multiple Wagering on more than two contestants a) Three Bets on the Same Contestant b) Three Simultaneous Bets on Different Contestants c) More than Simultaneous Bets, Flat and Plateau Wagering, Profit Taking a) Evaluating your Historical Bankroll Function, US Book g1631, **Casino Gambling for Winners!,** Moe Shuckelman, £5.99pb, 142pp, A parody of gambling books. It is intended to let you stop and look back at what gambling should really be. Fun - apparently, US Book

g1635, **Fixed: How Goodfellas Bought Boston College Basketball**, David Porter, £24.95hb, 256pp, Gambling scandal revolving round Boston College Basketball, US Book

g1636, **Games You Can't Lose,** £12.95pb, 160pp, Unveiling the tricks behind the cons, swindles and wagers that separate fools and their money, US Book

g1637, **Randomness,** Deborah J Bennett, £22.95hb, 238pp, Randomness explains probability and odds in an accessible way. It informs by recalling the real history of probability and solving many of its engaging puzzles., US book

g1639, **Adolescent Gambling** - Adolescence and Society Series, Mark Griffiths, £19.95pb, 304pp, Mark Griffiths has carried out extensive research into why some adolescents get hooked on gambling, how they gamble and what can be done about it. He provides an overview of adolescent gambling worldwide in additional to individual case studies, treatment approaches, and an insight into how the gaming industry induces young people to gamble, UK Book

g1642, **The Odds** - One Season, Three Gamblers and the Death of Their Las Vegas, Chad Millman, £26hb, 261pp, Milman tracks the fortunes of three punters during the march madness of the NCAA basketball tournament. This has become the biggest event for gamblers surpassing even the Super Bowl. Set against the a vivid portrait of a Las Vegas at the turn of the century, a city struggling to reconcile its lawless past, US Book

g1643, **Casino Gambling Made Easier**, Gayle Mitchell, £23.95pb, 107pp, How a rank amateur casino gambler can learn to win using intelligent gambling, US Book

g1644, **The Poker Club**, Ed Gorman, £5.99pb, 393pp, It all started so innocently. Just a group of friends meeting for the weekly poker game. Things took a murderous turn when an intruder broke in and was accidentally killed in the act by the poker buddies. They thought if they threw the body in the river no one would ever know. However the intruder was not alone and his accomplish had witnessed everything. Suddenly the game had changed. What had started out as a simple poker game now became a deadly game of cat and mouse, US Book

g1649, **Gambling Man**, Catherine Cookson, £4.99pb, 315pp, Rory Connor was a gambling man and he had a gambler's luck. From the day he was born, his mother had known that Rory would be the one to make something of his life. At seven years old he was earning money from odd jobs and by fourteen, he was in full-time work. By the time he was nineteen, he had escaped the factory to become a rent-collector. Now, at twenty-three, ambition was in full flow and he was always looking to bigger and better games to play. He feared nothing and nobody, not even the unscrupulous landlord he collected for. For an ordinary working lad, he was doing well - until one day, his luck changed and suddenly, things did not go as smoothly as he was Used to, UK Book

g1651, **Internet Gambling Report IV** - An Evolving Conflict Between Technology Policy & Law, Anthony Cabot, £60pb, 426pp, Approximately 30 additional pages and tons of updated information make this sixth edition of Cabot's book an important acquisition for anyone interested in all aspects of gambling and the internet. The 23 chapters are organized into the following basic headings: What is the Internet? What is Gambling? Can Gambling Work on the Internet? Traditional Vs. Internet Gambling; The Market: An Introduction; Let the Chips Fall: An Industry Begins to take Wing; Business Perspectives; Understanding Site Requirements; Keeping Things Secure; Developing Business; Protecting Your Property; Legal Regulatory and Policy Issues; Why Internet Gambling May Frustrate Public Policy; Prohibitory Challenges; Regulatory Challenges; United States; Native American Issues; Canada; European Overview; United Kingdom; France and Belgium; The Netherlands; Australia; Singapore; International Enforcement; Self-Regulation; Where From Here? Details in each section include items such as registration of players, legislation, unauthorized gambling; lotteries; gambling legislation, criminal jurisdiction; current federal (U.S.) law; ISP policing; government protection; even info on trademarks, domain names. From the book, this quote: This is a market with great growth potential. The numbers are seducing. Already the industry is realizing revenues of over 1.2 billion dollars. This is must-reading for lawyers, potential internet casino developers, current internet casino owners, and anyone interested in the ins and outs of internet gambling, US Book

GREYHOUND RACING

g234, **Greyhound Betting For Profit**, Ross Hamilton, £7.95pb, 64pp,
Takes the beginning bettor from the basics through every important factor
including post position, early speed, consistency, class, and the
quiniela, US Book

g294, **Greyhounds**, Roy Genders, £2.95pb, 101pp, A comprehensive
handbook for the prospective greyhound owner. Covers buying, feeding,
training, management and more, UK Book

g324, **Dogs: Homeopathic Remedies,** George Macleod, £6.95pb,
218pp, Covers all sorts of diseases, written by one of the few veterinary
surgeons to Use homeopathic medicines wholly and exclusively, UK Book

g425, **Adopting The Racing Greyhound**, Cynthia Brannigan, £9.95pb,
145pp, Chapters include: Choosing the Right Dog, The Racing Life, In a
Home, Care and Feeding, Insecticides and Anesthesia, and Training, US
Book

g535, **Greyhound Money Management For 90s**, Dan Casey, £10pb,
20pp, Defines poor money management, examines behaviour at windows, how to get value for money, betting capital, finding overlays,
and more, US Book

g538, **Winning With The Key Formula**, J M Hughes, £15.95pb, 43pp,
Complete course in understanding greyhounds including rating, understanding time and length relation, shippers, rules, speed, and sample
workout races, US Book

g539, **Winning Greyhound Handicapping**, Brian Mason, £15pb, 78pp,
For the more experienced player: focuses on back checking class, in-
grade analysis, shippers, favourites, throwing dogs out, isolating five
contenders etc, US Book

g550, **How To Bet Like A Pro At Dog Tracks**, John Page, £10pb, 39pp,
Discusses money management, systems, keeping accurate records, skip-
ping unbettable races, exactas, trifectas, etc, US Book

g607, **Winners Guide To Greyhound Racing**, Prof. Jones, £9.95pb,
96pp, This covers: Grades, Dogs Shipping in From Other Tracks, Recent
Form, Speed, Running Style, Kennels, Winning Analysis and Betting,
US Book

g619, **Dog Breeding**: Theory & Practice, Frank Jackson, £16.99pb,
208pp, Has chapters on: Genetics and Selection, Breeding Systems, The
Brood Bitch, The Stud Dog, Mating, Whelping, Post-Natal Care, Kennel
Management and more, UK Book

g653, **Complete Book Of Greyhounds**, Julia Barnes, £17.50pb, 238pp, Nice looking book which contains everything you need to know from the basics to racing. Lots of photos, UK Book

g846, **How To Analyze A Race,** Dan Casey, £10pb, 20pp, Breaks racing into five key factors, then presents a step by step approach to each factor with a sample race to be Used as practice., US Book

g862, **Homeopathic Medicine For Dogs**, Dr H G Wolff, £14.25pb, 228pp, A handbook for vets and owners., UK Book

g993, **Greyhound Tales**, Nora Star, £5pb, 116pp, Contains stories written by actual rescuers and adopters of greyhounds, US Book

g1010, **Pet Owners Guide To Greyhounds**, Anne Finch, £4.99pb, 80pp, Basic handbook with a lot of colour photos, UK Book

g1027, **Guide To Adopting Ex-Racing Greyhound**, Carolyn Raeke, £5.99pb, 64pp, Not very detailed, lots of colour pics. Covers History, Training, Grooming, Health, Feeding, and Temperament, US Book

g1303, **Gone To The Dogs,** Ron Duval, £14.95pb, 65pp, For beginners or intermediate players, with race examples, what to watch for when marking your programme, understanding terminology, keeping records etc, US Book

g1304, **The Greyhound Handicapper,** Earl Adams, £8.5pb, 70pp, How to read and correctly interpret key data from past performance record in the programme; identifying winning signals; ideas on watching odds board for smart money moves, and more, US Book

g1305, **Reign Of The Greyhou**nd, Cynthia Branigan, £24pb, 190pp, An in-depth history of the breed. Many photos, some in colour., US Book

g1310, **Advanced Handicap Rules & Reasons**, Don Casey, £10pb, 13pp, Two dozen ideas, angles, methods for the more knowledgeable bettor Includes why the one-eighth call is the key to winning races, learning the grading rules at tracks, and more, US Book

g1445, **How to Beat The Dog Races**, Bill McBride, £18.95pb, 176pp, Covers important ground for the novice and new territory for those who are more experienced, US Book

g1499, **Retired Racing Greyhounds for Dummies**, Lee Livingood, £14.99pb, 255pp, Are you thinking about adopting a retired racing Greyhound, or are you already sharing your life with one? This fun and friendly book is bursting with expert advice on all aspects of owning an ex-racer: understanding the Greyhound personality, taking care of your friend, teaching good manners, and much more. The author Lee Livingood has been training adult rescue dogs for nearly 40 years. She lives with two adopted ex-racers, volunteers for her Greyhound adoption group, and writes for Greyhound and other dog publications, US Book

g1501, **25 Articles** by Fred Brenner, Fred Brenner, £10pb, 30pp, Articles from a respected veteran covering such areas as marking your program, overemphasizing front-runners, pace and formula methods, US Book

g1334, **Irish Greyhound Review 2000**, Michael Fortune, £7pb, 128pp, A wealth of information about the Irish greyhound scene in 2000, UK Book

g1335, **The Irish Greyhound Derby. 1932-97**, Michael Fortune, £5pb, 96pp, Year by year account of ach derby, UK Book

g1353, **The Ultimate Greyhound**, Mark Sullivan, £25pb, 260pp, A guide to every aspect of the breed in the ULTIMATE series. A comprehensive health section is included along with over 200 illustrations, UK Book

G1663 , **The Book of the Greyhound**, Sue Le Mieux, £49.95 hb, 304pp. Comprehensive new book covering all facets of greyhounds from show champions to racers and adored pets. Illustrated with hundreds of colour photos and historical portraits.

Advance Notice — In November 2001 there will be a new UK Greyhound Betting Book called **The Pocket Essential Guide to Greyhound Racing** by V M Knight - it will retail at £3.99. Ring Scott on 020 7430 1021 for more details or to pre-order

HORSE RACING

g58, **Racetrack Betting**, Peter Asch, £19.95pb, 195pp, For the experienced bettor, this covers statistical models for place and show betting, the best way to overcome dismal statistics on exotic bets, US Book

g86, **Complete Pro Horse Race System**, W.J.Davies, £9.99pb, 176pp, A system based on having more than one horse working for you - for instance six. Whichever horse wins, you win the same amount of money, UK Book

g94, **Betting For A Living**, Nick Mordin, £18pb, 307pp, During the winter of 91/92 Mordin took £1000 a month off the bookies, betting mostly on bank holidays and weekends. This book tells the story, UK Book

g95, **The Winning Horseplayer**, Andrew Beyer, £14.00pb, 192pp, Offers the sophisticated bettor invaluable advice on topics like trip handicapping, track biases, the importance of pace etc. Beyer's books all sell well here, US Book

g153, **Overlay,**   Overlay: How To Bet Horses, Bill Heller, £8.99pb, 228pp, Overlays are horses that pay more than they should. Heller Uses sound handicapping advice that can be used at any racetrack. No elaborate point systems or gimmicks, US Book

g158, **Woulda, Coulda, Shoulda**, David Feldman, £12.95pb, 294pp, Veteran handicapper, columnist, and stable owner, explores the principles of handicapping in 10 chapters. Some good photos and a sense of humour too!, US Book

g210, **The Punters Friend**, Jack Waterman, 12.99pb, 306pp, A handbook and guide to horse-racing and the language of book-making, UK Book

g172, **Alex Bird**: Life & Secrets Of, Bird & Manners, £15.99pb, 256pp, Excellent biography of legendary gambler. Another book with limited stock, UK Book

g288, **Value Factor In Successful Betting**, Malcolm Howard, £5.95pb, 110pp, Published in 1991, this covers: assessing risk, hazards of handicapping, choosing the right races, preparing the actual race profile, sensible betting strategies etc, UK Book

g301, **Payday At The Races**, Les Conklin, £7pb, 208pp, Deals with the very basics of handicapping then moves to a systems section. Also, why certain things happen and how you can predict them, or stay away, US Book

g302, **Betting Horses To Win**, Les Conklin, £8.95pb, 183pp, Five major sections cover Power Plays, Borderline Cases, Betting Methods, Best Bets, and the Second Year. First published in 1954, US Book

g306, **150 Blue Ribbon Winning Systems**, GBC Staff, £4.95pb, 64pp, A collection of prize thoroughbred systems and methods: includes speed, weight, 2 year olds, and claimers, US Book

g313, **Eliminate Losers: Pick The Winners**, Bob McKnight, £5pb, 189pp, Through hard work and diligence, learning and considering condition, class, percentages, distances, and several other concepts, you'll start to win, this one says, US Book

g354, **License To Print Money**, Jamie Reid, £8.99pb, 272pp, Takes a look at the codes and practises that make up the betting industry. One of the best racing/gambling accounts of recent years, UK Book

g364, **Win At All Weather Racing**, Tony Stafford, £3.25pb, 48pp, This is the first publication to give exclusive attention to betting profitably on All-Weather Track Racing. Published in 1991, UK Book

g369, **How To Win At Racing**, Spectator, £2.95pb, 47pp, How to study form in all its many aspects and how to apply it to finding winners is the main theme of this one. Breeding, jockeyship, paddock inspection etc., UK Book

g371, **Vincent O'Brien, Man And Legend**, Raymond Smith, £9.95pb, 270pp, In-depth biography of the Worlds Greatest Trainer, UK Book

g403, **Ainslie's Complete Guide To Thoroughbreds**, Tom Ainslie, £13pb, 348pp, An American racing classic that has been selling for over twenty years, This third edition adds features such as Studying horses in paddock and post parade. 60 principles to build your own system. Judging jockeys and trainers. Understanding the mystery of breeding. Behind the scenes at the racetrac., US Book

g419, **How To Win At Horseracing**, Robert Rowe, £9.95pb, 200pp, A seasoned pro reveals his methods of evaluating trainers and jockeys, how to make money with the top three favourites, get the best payoffs and more, US Book

g469, **Body Language Of Horses,** Ainslie & Ledbetter, £19.95pb, 204pp, Revealing the nature of equine needs wishes and emotions, and how horses communicate them. For owners, breeders, trainers, riders, and other horse lovers, US Book

g470, **Picking Winners**, Andrew Beyer, £14pb, 224pp, Covering such topics as the joy of handicapping, larceny and betting coups, speed handicapping and more, this is the classic 1975 book updated, US Book g481, **Always Back Winners**, Stewart Simpson, £9.99pb, 159pp, Since it was published in 1981, the book has established a well-earned cult following amongst system backers and this latest reprint is not edited or updates - it doesn't need to be. It simply allows you to gain access to a system which has stood the test of time and is as successful now as it has ever been., UK Book

g490, **Money Secrets Of The Racetrack**, Barry Meadow, £24.95pb, 148pp, Excellent book on money management along with Commonsense Betting. Designed for the U.S. tote system, so the detailed strategies work even better in GB where you can take a price with the bookmakers., US Book

g492, **100 Hints For Better Betting**, Mark Coton, £11.95pb, 125pp, A look inside the mind of the professional gambler, and examines all stages of the betting process, from preparing selections to accurate and consistent staking, UK Book

g563, **Training Thoroughbred Horses**, Preston Burch, £19.95pb, 119pp, Learn how to: select good stock, condition each horse individually, place each horse where it can win, treat minor injuries etc., US Book

g575, **Training The Racehorse**, Fitzgeorge-Parker, £15.95pb, 258pp, First published in 1976 and widely considered the standard work in its field. Information on finding, breaking, training, and placing racehorses, UK Book

g578, **Mozans Racing Numerology**, Mozan, £2.95pb, 71pp, A how-to-pick winners book Using what is called 'the science of numbers.' No consideration of form, breeding, conditions, speed etc, US Book

g584, **Racing Maxims Pittsburgh Phil**, Edward Cole, £7.95pb, 126pp, 1908 classic of the only interview the legendary plunger gave. Sharp observations on handicapping that are still timely today. Sells well, US Book

g589, **Betting The Timeform Way**, Timeform, £9.95pb, 96pp, Concentrates on the mathematical side of racing and demonstrates that a probable winner and a betting opportunity aren't one and the same, UK Book

g592, **Winning In The 90,** Joe Takach, £32pb, 201pp, For the serious player. Sections on the 'ready horse', the warm-up, the 'fit' racehorse, the also-rans the sore horse, the ill horse, the drugged horse and more., US Book

g596, **Betting Thoroughbreds**, Steve Davidowitz, £16.95pb, 345pp, Known as the sourcebook to serious handicappers, this American classic guide now features groundbreaking chapters on pace analysis; innovative approaches to handicapping, claiming, allowance races at major and minor tracks, new ways to use workout and breeding information, US Book

44

g644, **How Will Your Horse Run Today?**, William L. Scott, £9.95pb, 210pp, Published in 1981, Scott concentrates on current form exclusively. Analysing workouts, last race recency analysing last race running lines, performance within the form cycle etc, US Book

g660, **Dutching Made Simple**, Jim Giordano, £6.95pb, 13pp, A slim little number that contains a simple and accurate method for playing any number of horses or exacta combinations in one race, US Book

g669, **Postures, Profiles and Performance**, Joe Takach, £29.95pb, 139pp, Knowing when a horse is physically fit is as important as how to bet when you've isolated a solid contender. Discusses lasix profiles, circling, bobbing, dropped heads and more. US Book

g680, **150 More Blue Ribbon Winning System**, GBC Staff, £4.95pb, 64pp, This one concentrates on long-shots, money management, consensus, class and claiming races, US Book

g697, **Handicapper's Stakes Festival,** James Quinn, £25pb, 314pp, An in-depth look at simulcasting, satellite wagering, and stakes festivals. He analyses effective handicapping in stakes races, and more, US Book

g712, **Racing Ready Reckoner**, Sharpe & Frater, £4.99pb, 165pp, Includes: the settlement of all standard bets, chart which shows odds as a percentage, how to make a 'book', a Tic Tac sign language chart of all major prices etc. UK Book

g721, **Art and Science Racehorse Training**, Michael Marshall, £14.95pb, 179pp, Bill Marshall has trained racehorses across four continents. Covers all aspects of racehorse training, from the basics to advanced levels., UK Book

g745, **25 Ways To Beat The Horses**, Walter B.Gibson, £8.95pb, 140pp, Betting formulas from a turf authority for Use when playing favourites, middle odds, and long shots. Covers all aspects of picking the winners., US Book

g774, **Race Is Pace**, Huey Mahl, £7.95pb, 126pp, Discusses odds, the importance of horse power, physiology and fitness, the conditions of eligibility, the speed vs pace controversy, and condition and variant, US Book

g788, **Come Fly With The Butterfly**, John Mort Green, £9.99pb, 127pp, The 10 secrets of successful punting written by one of the most successful pro punters. We have a limited stock of this one—still, UK Book

g795, **Situation Handicapping**, Joe Takach, £29.95pb, 158pp, Includes discussions of Lasix, prerace warm-ups, the ready horse off a lay-off,

off a claim, stretching out. Despite the price Takach sells well, US Book

g801, **Winning Strategies & Ready Horse**, Joe Takach, £32pb, 204pp, Focuses how to keep a winning stable of racehorses (on paper, not buying them) and concentrates on a dozen key factors to look for in a thoroughbred, US Book

g804, **Beyer On Speed,** Andy Beyer, £14pb, 238pp, Another Beyer bestseller. Shows how to make speed the focal point of an effective strategy for race track betting. First published in 1993, US Book

g808, **Handicap Finding The Key Horse,** David Christopher, £12.95pb, 166pp, Offers a reliable way to identify the three or four most promising contenders in any race, and several profitable methods for selecting a Key Horse, US Book

g813, **Total Victory At The Track**, William Scott, £12.95pb, 288pp, Concentrates on the concept of Performance Class Ratings, also How to Make Class Determinations, Vital Form Factors, the Track Variant and more, US Book

g814, **Horses Talk: It Pays To Listen**, Trillis Parker, £19.95pb, 194pp, For the serious horse player: about Paddock and Post Parade Inspection, signposts to longshots, with detailed descriptions and detailed drawings. Sells very well, US Book

g816, **Against The Crowd**, Alan Potts, £8.95pb, 124pp, The methods of a modern backer. Potts reveals the techniques and methods that give him the edge over bookmakers, UK Book

g839, **Phil Bull**: The Biography, Howard Wright, £18.95pb, 331pp, The first biog' of the man who made a fortune out of betting on horses, and was also a successful breeder and owner, UK Book

g847, **Expert Handicapping,** Dave Litfin, £24.95pb, 294pp, Winning insights into betting thoroughbreds. Examines hundreds of races and result charts and offers examples of situations, strategies, trends which may continue, US Book

g858, **Exploring Pedigree**, Mike Helm, £29.95pb, 223pp, State of the art pedigree info' and a proven perspective on how to use it. Allows handicappers to evaluate debut runners in Maiden races and more, US Book

g911, **Better One Day As A Lion**, Raymond Smith, £9.95pb, 261pp, Has three main sections. The first covers jump trainers and jockeys, the second men of the flat, and finally some high rollers who never lived like lambs!, UK Book

g922, **Jump Racing For Profit**, Peter May, £3.95pb, 36pp, May is a professional computer analyst of many years experience. Here he applies the results of massive statistical research for another excellent book., UK Book

g962, **How To Compile Your Own Handicap**, David Dickinson, £9.95pb, 128pp, Covers the rules you should follow, getting started, and day to day running. Also the role of the clock, and Dickinson's views on betting., UK Book

g969, **Odds Must Be Crazy**, Len Ragozin, £23.95pb, 314pp, Beating the races with the man who revolutionized handicapping. Explains the systems that made him famous. Sells well, US Book

g994, **Real Life Handicapping**, Dave Litfin, £24.95pb, 189pp, Persuasively shows that eclectic players who combine an intimate knowledge of at least one track stand the best chance of success. Other topics discussed too, US Book

g1030, **Winning Horse Racing Formula**, David Duncan, £6.99pb, 125pp, The 12 golden rules of successful betting: stake right, win more lose less: 7 steps to a better selection strategy. UK Book

g1063, **More Dark Secrets Of The Turf**, John White, £11.99pb, 183pp, Over 40 betting strategies and packed with lots of other Useful info. , UK Book

g1064, **Inside Track**, Alan Potts, £18pb, 255pp, Describes the methods Potts Used to generate over ?50, 000 profit from his betting during 1997 UK Book

g1102, **Formsires**, Laurence Taylor, £9.95pb, 136pp, Written by the man who edits the High Stakes magazine this is a study of pedigree handicapping which enables you to stay ahead of the crowd. Buy lots!, UK Book

g1103, **Idiots Guide Betting On Horses**, Sharon B Smith, £10.99pb, 268pp, Comprehensive, well laid out book for the beginner and for those with experience. Covers just about everything, plus diagrams and photos., US Book

g1119, **The Racing World Of Damon Runyon**, Damon Runyon, £14.99pb, 170pp, A collection of Runyon's writing from the 1920's, concerning small-time hustlers and impecunious trainers from the racetracks of York and Florida, US Book

g1121, **The War Zone**, Pippy, £4.95pb, 63pp, The War Zone is the betting shop, and Pippy shows the punter how he can get on top. Pinpoints bets to go for and ones to avoid, and which bookies offer best value in exotic bets, UK Book g1127, **Giving A Little Ba**ck, Barney Curley, £15.99pb, 279pp, Autobiography of famous and hugely successful punter, including one scam in which he relieved the bookmakers of £300,000, UK Book

g1138, **Channel 4 Racing Form & Betting**, John Mccririck, £5.99pb, 125pp, Guide to form and betting from Channel 4 team. Recently updated, UK Book

g1144, **Thoroughbred Business Guide**, Paddy Finlason, £15pb, 340pp, Excellent directory of over 4, 500 people and companies involved in the UK and Irish racing and breeding industries. Also with racing diary and studs info'., UK Book

g1154, **How To Pick Winners**, Al Illich, £12pb, 202pp, Well known turf operator, publishes for the first time his proven theories and systems, covering every important aspect of betting on the flats and the trotters., US Book

g1155, **Exotic Overlays**, Bill Heller, £14.95pb, 221pp, How to get BIG payoffs from the Pick Six, the Pick Three, exactas, triples, doubles, and superfectas, US Book

g1157, **Prime Collection,** Joe Takach, £29.95pb, 137pp, A collection of Takash's 42 best articles from handicapping letters like The Inside Track, and the Cramer-Olmsted Report, US Book

g1158, **Teach Yourself: Horse Racing**, Belinda Levez, £4.99pb, 86pp, Short handbook for beginners. Covers off-course betting, tote betting, bookmaking, betting strategies and ready reckoner, US Book

g1177, **Travelling The Turf. 15th Ed**, Julian West, £15pb, 304pp, Complete guide to the racecourses of GB and Ireland, plus some international. Complete racing calendar also included. Lavishly illustrated, with other articles too. HB available at 17.99, UK Book

g1187, **An Arm And Four Legs**, Stan Hey, £8pb, 230pp, A journey into racehorse ownership. Hey has painted a vivid and humoroUS picture of the inner circle of National Hunt racing from the owners point of view. , UK Book

g1191, **Thoroughbred Handicapping**, The Computer Way, Howard Berenbon, £19.95pb, 65pp, A program for handicapping that works for PC and Apple models. Also a spreadsheet handicapping system for Use in Lotus, Excel, Quattro Pro, and one formula/system for a pocket calculator, US Book

g1192, **Value Handicapping**, Mark Cramer, £24pb, 165pp, This pioneering work concentrates on showing the handicapper how to create a personal odds line and Use it to identify which horses are overlays and worth consideration for a wager. Plus more, US Book

g1197, **Turf Overlays**, Bill Heller, £12.95pb, 112pp, Looks at which trainers and jockeys do better on grass than dirt. Lists every mare who produced a major stakes winner anywhere in the world in 96-97, US Book

g1198, **How To Win At Thoroughbred Racing**, Robert Rowe, £24pb, 60pp, Handicapping procedures to find overlays. In 10 lessons Rowe establishes a standardised approach to finding selections with superior percentage-of-return records, US Book

g1202, **Trackfacts**, Dan Dipleco, £24.95pb, 170pp, This is filled with handicappers questions and answers based on data analysis of more than 100,000 bits of research. 8 major sections Using charts and graphs, US Book

g1207, **Wire Em And Win**, Denny Border, £12.95pb, 119pp, Includes optimum application of speed figures, explains all types of pari-mutuel wagers, expounds on the daily double, pick-3 and other exotic wagers, plus more, US Book

g1223, **Channel 4 Guide To Racehorses**, £9.99pb, 168pp, What to look for in a horse; explains the breeding business and history of Thoroughbreds. Also describes the routine of training, injuries etc. , UK Book

g1249, **Betting Market As A Guide To Winners,** Malcolm Howard, £9.95pb, 80pp, An overview of the racing and betting markets, how to use the market as a guide, market form for over 500 horses, UK Book

g1265, **Trip Tips**, Joe Takach, £29.95pb, 140pp, For serious handicappers who know that horses who have a bad 'trip' in one race may very well succeed in their next if you look at analysis and make observations, US Book

g1267, **The Racing Tribe,** Kate Fox, £17.99pb, 256pp, This is an inside look at the racing world by a social anthropologist who has also written with Desmond Morris. With 32 pages of photos, UK Book

g1295, **200% Of Nothing**, A. K. Dewdney, £14.95pb, 182pp, Under an umbrella that covers countless examples of 'innumeracy' the author details some shocking discoveries made by 'mathematics abuse detectives'. Takes the lid off traditional statistics, US Book

g1311, **Pocket Idiots Guide Horse Betting**, Sharon B.Smith, £5.99pb, 216pp, A smaller version of the larger Idiots Guide. Nicely done, US Book

g1312, **Tote Guide To Horseracing & Betting**, Helen Parker, £4.99pb, 144pp, Handy pocket guide to all 59 racecourses in Britain. How to get there, what they cost, where to drink, etc. Also available in small hardback for 6.99, UK Book

g1321, Crossing The Line, Charlie Brooks, £7.99pb, 311pp, Charlie Brooks is one of the most dashing characters on the racing scene and until spring 1998 he was a leading trainer. The future looked dazzling until in a flurry of publicity and rumour, Charlie Brooks became an ex-trainer Then came a fateful Friday in January 1999 when he was arrested in connection with the long-running police investigation into race fixing. Freed from the shackles of having to conform to the Turf's code of what can and cannot be told, the author takes the lid off the racing world to provide a candid commentary on the state of the sport today and what is going on behind closed stable doors. He has crossed the line from insider to outsider, and that is his uniquely informed and honest view of the weird and wonderful world of British horse racing, UK Book

g1342, Bloodstock Breeding, Charles Leicester, £30pb, 505pp, Information and ideas which are of importance and practical Usefulness not only to thoroughbred breeders, owners and trainers but to anyone with a serious interest in the racehorse, US Book

g1359, Body Language Columns, Trillis Parker, £19.95sb, 96pp, This is a collection of columns written by the author for the Racing Times covering a variety of body movements and changes on the racing thoroughbred that can be used to determine whether or not the horse is ready, US Book

g1381, High Rollers of the Turf - Millennium Edition, Raymond Smith, £9.99pb, 280pp, This fascinating book gives revealing insights into the world of the High Rollers. They're all here, the big hitters the bookies fear like J.P. (The Sundance Kid) McManus, Michael Tabor and Barney Curley. The full story is told of how Noel Furlong, famous for his £4 million double bid at Cheltenham '91, took the Las Vegas scene by storm by winning the 1999 World Hold'em Poker Championship, bringing home to Ireland a cool $1 million, UK Book

g1382, Ultimate Dream: 75 Years of the Tote Cheltenham Gold Cup, Bob Harman, £7.99pb, 222pp, Since its humble inception way back in 1924, the Cheltenham Gold Cup has grown in status and popularity and is now widely regarded as the world's greatest steeplechase. Climbing the famous Cheltenham hill to victory has been compared to reaching the peak of Everest or - in the words of Jonjo O'Neill, who rode 1986 winner Dawn Run trying to get to Heaven Over the years, Gold Cup winners have come in all shapes, sizes and colours. Memorable highlights include Golden Miller's unparalleled five successive wins from 1932 to 1936, the incredible Michael Dickinson-trained 1-2-3-4-5 of 1983, and latterly, the ever-popular Desert Orchid, whose 1989 victory typified the battling qualities needed to be a champion., UK Book

g1385, Backing the Draw for Profit, Graham Weldon, £9.95pb, 109pp, On many British racecourses, the draw has more influence on the outcome of the races than any other single factor. In fact, it is possible to make a healthy profit simply by backing well-drawn horses. This book shows you how a profit can be made from this most crucial factor, UK Book

g1386, **New Form Sires for the Millennium**: Breeding as a Guide to Winners, Lawrence Taylor, £9.95pb, 128pp, Updated version of Taylor's popular book Form Sires on breeding as a guide to winners, UK Book

g1387, **Sprint Handicaps Explained**, Jim Adams, £9.95pb, 128pp, An introduction to the fascinating art of handicapping, taken step by step through last season's 5f and 6f races, UK Book

g1388, **Trendsetters Review for the Flat**: A Statistical Guide to 110 Major Races, Andrew Ayres, £9.95pb, 128pp, A ten year analysis of the tends which have been established in 111 major races, UK Book

g1400, **Horse Racing**: The Essential Guide to Backing Winners, Sidney Harris , £18pb, 95pp, Cuts out the painful process of having to encounter the pitfalls and goes on to enlighten the student in a clear and instructive way, Recommended, UK Book

g1407, **Laughing in the Hills**, Bill Barich , £14pb, 228pp, Barich debuted in 1980 with this magnificent meditation on horse-racing, yet the rich, full portrait he paints of the track and its colourful citizenry--human and hoofed--is only prelude to the work's enduring appeal. It is really a finely crafted memoir about loss and longing, renewal and affirmation, US Book

g1408, **Racing Man's Bedside Book** , Julian Bedford , £18.95pb, 212pp, A bedside book of racing stories, anecdotes, reminiscences, poems and observations as varied and rich as the racing scene itself. The six sections in the book encompass Horses, Owners, Trainers, Jockeys, The Players and the great Racing Festivals, UK Book

g1426, **The Book on Bookies**, James Jefferies , £18pb, 152pp, If you have ever wondered why the bookie always wins and you always lose, or how your bookie adjusts point spreads and in which direction, The Book on Bookies is for you. In it, you'll find all the answers you need to come out a winner, no matter what you bet on - football, baseball, horse racing, boxing, golf or any other sport. Go behind the scenes with J.J. to see how a professional sports book is set up and run. Find out all about point spreads, straight bets, half-points, parlays, exactas, teasers, exotics, sweeps money lines - everything you need to know to wager wisely . . . or to become a bookie! , US Book

g1439, **Daily Telegraph Pocket Racing Guide**: The Inside Track on Horseracing, £9.99pb, 224pp, Useful new overview of the industry including chapter on Betting in the New Millennium, UK Book g1448, **The Top 52,** Len Czyzniejewski, £39sp, 118pp, This is a consumer-oriented test of fifty-two commercially-available horseracing systems with an undeniably US bias, US Book

g1455, **Turf-Moms**, £60sp, 272pp, A database which tries to prove that the power of the dam to be the basis upon which handicapping decisions, based on breeding alone, can be made with assurance and confidence, US Book

g1473, **Matriarchs: Great Mares of the 20th Century**, Edward L. Bowen, £34.95hb, 223pp, A definitive look at a select group of these top American broodmares and their descendants. What these mares all have in common, however, is their lasting influence on the Thoroughbred breed, US Book

g1478, **Language of Horse Racing** , Gerald Hammond, £35hb, 244pp, Offers a new conception and analysis of the vocabulary Used in our sports. Contains an essential lexicon of words and phrases - explored historically and in depth each also contains generous quotation, practical reference, anecdote and conjecture, US Book

g1480, **Judgement of Form**, Marvex, £10pb, 38pp, Includes Form Book, Class, Breeding, Race to avoid, Time of the Year, Sentiment in Racing, The apprentice Allowance, The Handicap, the Scale of Weight for Age, National Hunt Racing, Win or Each Way, Interlude, The Last Act, UK Book

g1482, **Betting for Profit**, Marvex, £10pb, 42pp, The first book on betting written on 1948 by Marvex, an accountant with a penchant for getting to the nitty-gritty in an interesting and absorbing way. In this book he gives his thought on all the important aspects of winner finding and even the widest-read punter will find at least one other slant on racing matters, UK Book

g1483, **Searching for a System:** The Science of Systems - Volume 1, Tony Peach , £7.5pb, 26pp, Collection of articles about systems, UK Book

g1484, **Planning a Better Bet:** The Science of Systems - Volume 2, Tony Peach , £10pb, 30pp, Various ways of searching out and improving systematic betting., UK Book

g1485, **Beating the Book**: The Science of Systems - Volume 3, Tony Peach, £10pb, 30pp, Tony Peach sets down in easy terms how to go about finding out whether the odds are Value for Money through Beating The Book a revised version of the 1989 edition of The Punters Books, which is now out of print, UK Book

g1487, **Ultimate Wheil of Fortune**, Tony Peach, £7.5pb, 38pp, Six remaining articles VDW wrote for the Handicap Book and Raceform Update from 1981 to 1986, UK Book

g1488, **Betting the VDW Way**, edited, Tony Peach , £7.5pb, 30pp, VDW articles reprinted from out of print books Winning Ways to Bet, Make Racing Play Volume 2 and Systematic Betting, UK Book

g1489, **The Golden Years of Van Der Wheil**: Tribute to VDW 1978-1982, edited, Tony Peach, £10pb, 42pp, A collection of the legendary Flying Dutchman's letters which chronicles his methods of finding winners, UK Book

g1490, **Racing in my System**, Tony Peach , £6pb, 42pp, Tony Peach talks to and about Che Van Der Wheil, who also pens another article for the author, Tony Peach writes several chapters on past systems he highlighted in Sports Forum, UK Book

g1491, **Champion Charlie**, Michael Clower, £7.99pb, 224pp, Charlie Swan was Ireland's champion jump jockey for nine consecutive seasons and he has ridden more National Hunt winners in Ireland than any other jockey in history. He holds the Irish records for both the most winners in a season and the most in a calendar year. He has twice been leading jockey at the Cheltenham Festival and has a string of big-race victories to his credit including two Champion Hurdles, the Queen Mother Champion Chase, the Irish Grand National, two Whitbread Gold Cups and four Irish Champion Hurdles. But life has been far from easy for Charlie Swan. This absorbing book relates how he has had to struggle in his early years as an apprentice and describes the terrible toll racing has taken on him physically. This book does much more than tell the life story of a brave and brilliant jockey. By revealing the aims and ambitions of the trainers with whom Swan has been most closely associated - men such as Edward O'Grady, Tom Foley and Aidan O'Brien - as well as their setbacks and disappointments, he brings the world of racing vividly to life, UK Book

g1492, **Newmarket: From James I to the Present Day**, Laura Thompson, £20hb, 341pp, From the author of The Dogs, here Laura Thompson looks into the life of market, past and present, and reveals a portrait of the town that is both authoritative and informal. Her passion for the sport - for its romance, its glamour, its excitement, but also for its resolutely undemocratic nature - makes this a unique and entertaining history, UK Book

g1493, **The Boss: The Life and Times of Horseracing Legend Gordon W.Richards**, John Budden, £15.99hb, 237pp, Charts the successes of the man who twice saddled more than a hundred winners in a single season and who scooped the pool in the Aintree Grand National on two occasions. This enthralling biography, written with the full co-operation of Richards himself, provides a compelling insight into the forces that drove him to become of the most respected trainers in the world, UK Book g1512, **Superform Races and Racehorses Jump Racing 2000 Edition,** £23.5pb, 1312pp, Results , Ratings and Commentaries for Jump Racing from June 4th 1999 - July 17th 2000, UK Book

g1515, **100 Jumpers to Follow 2000-2001,** £3.50pb, 48pp, Thirty-eighth year of publication and a companion volume to 100 Winners on the Flat, UK Book

g1525, **Gold from the Sand** - The Alchemy of All-Weather Racing, David Bellingham, £9.95pb, 128pp, All-weather racing began in 1989 at the Equitrack at Lingfield. Through the Use of personal anecdotes and experience gained over the years, together with some statistics, the author helps make the All-Weather picture that much clearer by setting out a strategy which help give readers an edge over their fellow punters. He argues that All-Weather racing should be treated as a separate entity rather than merely the poor relation of the turf and, in any case, backing a winner gives the same buzz irrespective of the type of surface the horse ran on. Recommended, UK Book

g1532, **Gallant Sport** - The Authentic History of Liverpool Races and the Grand National, John Pinford, £26hb, 296pp, Although there have been many books about the Grand National, none has had access to all the sources used for this authentic history of the origins of the world's greatest steeplechase. Drawing in particular from contemporary newspaper files and from the papers of the Earls of Sefton, Gallant Sport reveals many new aspects of the Grand National story. Standard histories, nearly all of them based on sources which date from long after the events they describe, give 1839 as the date the National was first run at Aintree, and Lottery as the first winner. This book proves that the first Grand national took place not in 1839, nor in 1837, but in 1836, and that the race - won by The Duke ridden by Captain Becher - and all the subsequent ones, took place over a course which was in all essentials the same as the one in use today. This discovery, along with many others by author John Pinfold (including previously unknown illustrations), makes this book an important work in itself. It is also a splendidly entertaining book, putting racing history in the broader context of social history with its many colourful stories from Aintree's past. Produced and presented to the Usual high standard associated with Portway Press this would make an impressive Christmas gift, UK Book

g1533, **National Hunt Dark Horses 2000 - 2001,** Marten Julian, £4.99pb, 107pp, An old classic now in a different, more user friendly format. The purpose of this book is to provide punters with information about unexposed horses. That is why there is only passing reference to National Hunt racing's leading stars. Includes The Northern Notebook, The Long and Winding Road, The Southern Selections, Track Trends and a Useful index for the hundred horses featured, UK Book

g1534, **Obsessed** - The Autobiography, Richard Dunwoody, £18.99hb,

294pp, Obsessed is the story of a jump jockey and his compulsion to be the best. The rewards were huge including guiding West Tip to victory in the 1986 Grand National at the astonishingly young age of 22. However the downside of his successes are not so well documented, UK Book

g1535, **Two-Year-Old Review Of 2000**, Peter May, £6.95pb, 88pp, Includes overview of the ratings, summary of the 2000 season, Sire analysis for 2000 by Going, Sires analysis for 2000 for Distance, Sires analysis for 2000 by month, winners of the main 2-y.o races, Top 40 juveniles of 2000, race distance analysis for 2000, trainer analysis for 2000, Sires of British Group Race winners 1996-2000, 1, 000 Guineas Preview, 2, 000 Guineas Preview, 2-y.o Turf Ratings of 2000, Analysis of 2-y.o winners of 2000., UK Book

g1537, **Dick Hern**, Peter Willett, £18.99hb, 293pp, The long-awaited official biography of one of the most successful racehorse trainers ever. Champion trainer four times, Dick Hern has an unsurpassed reputation as a trainer of classic horses. He has won an exceptional sixteen British classic races, including the Derby with Troy, Henbit and Nashwan. In addition he trained the supremely talented Brigadier Gerard, who has been described as the British horse of the 20th century and who won seventeen of his eighteen races. Hern is an unusually colourful character with a distinguished war record and an extremely interesting life, UK Book

g1539, **Winning Turf Strategy**, £49.95pb, 40pp, Picking turf winners is one of the hardest parts of the game for some handicappers, particularly at tracks that have only one race a day on that kind of surface. In this book, the author, who is widely known in the modern handicapping arena, takes a specialized look at several different strategies to help you handicap races on the grass, US Book

g1544, **The Wayward Lad** - The Autobiography of Graham Bradley, Graham Bradley, £17.99hb, 440pp, Controversy and Graham Bradley have ridden side by side throughout his 23 year career as one of the most charismatic jump jockeys that Britain has ever seen. As he fought his way from a council estate in West Yorkshire to ride for the finest stables in Britain and Ireland he made headlines - and not always for the right reasons. He talks candidly about his life as one of the great jockeys and he interweaves this with his account of the dawn raid by the Serious Crime Squad and the daunting period he spent under suspicion, Damn good read, UK Book

g1559, **Horse Racing Legends** - Calendar 2001,£7.99, Calendar, UK Calendar

g1564, **Welsh Grand National 1895-1999** - The Complete Record - Issue 22, Paul Davies, £5pb, 38pp, The Complete Record is a statistical review of the leading National Hunt races. It is invaluable to students of the turf history, statisticians and for betting purposes, showing up the trends of previous renewals of particular races. Each issue contains: Year-by-year results with finishing order, age and weight, trainer and jockey Index to every horse to run in the race Extensive career histories of every winning horse Full records of every trainer and jockey A complete history The French and Irish challenge The supporting races reviewed in detail A comprehensive betting guide Race Records, UK Book

g1565, **Lightning in a Jar**, W. Campbell, £29.95hb, 310pp, The ins and outs of owning a thoroughbred racehorse as author W. Cothran Campbell demystifies the ownership process through a unique combination of how-to guide and autobiography, US Book

g1567, **Flat Annual for 2001** - The Official Form Book (All the 2000 Returns), Raceform, £25pb, 1900pp, Complete record of all Flat Racing from November 7th, 1999 to November 4th, 2000, UK Book

g1570, **Memoirs of a Mug Punter**, John Harm, £12.95pb, 237pp, John Harms' second book after his account of an Ashes series Confessions of a Third Man. Here Harms' joined a syndicate intent on proving that anyone can own a racehorse. The mare Courting Pleasure didn't seem to adhere to this philosophy. This is a tale of jockeys and trainers, bookies and strappers and along with these people a fable about obsessive hope and manic despair, UK Book

g1575, **Handicapping in Cyberspace** - The Horseplayer's Complete Guide to the Internet, George Kaywood, £29.95sp, 239pp, The Horseplayer's Complete Guide to the Internet, US Book/CD Rom

g1580, **Speed and the Thoroughbred**: The Complete History , Alexander Mackay-Smith, £50hb, 193pp, It has been said that the invention of the Thoroughbred was the single most consequential turning point in the evolution of the horse since its domestication. Its blood has provided the key to superiority in nearly every equestrian discipline. What the Thoroughbred has created, how, by whom, and how its progenitors survived war, politics, and the ambitions and jealousies of monarchs, noblemen, and politicians is the subject of this book. Handsomely illustrated with paintings and photographs and more than 10 years in the making, this is the first book to identify and historically trace the three sources of Thoroughbred speed; the pre-Christian Irish hobby, the sixteenth-century English running-Horse, and a few Middle-Eastern imports, US Book

g1582, **Make Money with Horses**, Don Blazer, £19.95pb, 157pp, This new edition Includes syndication guidelines. A practical workbook which explains the facets of the horse industry, and tells in simple terms exactly what it takes to make big profits. Different from most guides, make money with horses gives you the absolute rules to be successful, US Book

g1593, **Modern Pace Handicapping**, Tom Brohamer, £25hb, 288pp, Revised and Updated edition. In Modern pace handicapping illustrates that fractional times, running styles, turn-times, track variants and final times are all interrelated and not independent factors when it comes to pace handicapping. The handicapping puzzle is most easily solved within the relationships between these various factors. The handicapper is taught to match running styles and pace preferences to track profiles and decision models, thus gaining a significant edge on the crowd. the material in this book is not easy. But it works. Handicappers willing to persevere will find it well worthwhile. Recommended, US Book

g1596, **Superform Races and Racehorses Flat Edition - 2001**, £24.99pb, 1724pp, Results, Ratings and Commentaries for Flat Racing, Turf and All Weather from November 8th 1999 - November 4th 2000, UK Book

g1597, **Handicapper's Condition Book** - An Advanced Treatment of Thoroughbred Class, James Quinn, £29.95hb, 208pp, Modern handicappers who rely on traditional standards of class appraisal are beset by radically changing of play, including purse inflation, year-round calendars, emphasis on younger horses, and a proliferation of stake races. In this revised and updated version of the handicapping classic, James Quinn shows how to relate past performances to the class demands of eligibility conditions that are standard fare in major racing and provides selection and elimination guidelines that handicappers can use to isolate horses well suited to particular races. Part One discusses the full array of race conditions in a progression that most thoroughbred follow, from maiden to claiming races. The revised and updated section on stakes races features the increasingly important role of international racing. Part Two concentrates on developing horses, notably nonclaiming three-year-olds, urging handicappers to rely on in-depth comprehension of eligibility conditions and well-known patterns of development when the past performances do not yet tell a persuasive story. Included are two appendices, one of the selection-elimination guidelines and the other, recently updated Beyer Speed Figure par charts for major, midlevel and minor tracks, UK Book

g1609, **Legend of Istabraq**, Michael Clower, £15.99hb, 168pp, Istabraq is one of the greatest hurdlers of all time, only the fifth horse in racing history to win three consecutive Champion Hurdles, and with the legendary Arkle and Golden Miller, one of only three horses to win at four Cheltenham Festivals in a row. However, The legends of Istabraq is much more than the story of a famous racehorse. Beneath the big race glory is the tragedy of a man who first recognised Istabraq's phenomenal potential. John Durkan persuaded the legendary gambler J.P. McManus to but the horse, who he believed would launch his own training career. Tragically, Durkan was struck down by leukaemia and was forced to follow the horse's early jumping career from a hospital bed as he fought to contain the illness which eventually killed him. , UK Book

g1616, **Flat Racing and British Society 1790-1914**: A Social and Economic History, Mike Huggins, £19.95pb, 270pp, This is the first detailed study of the formative period of flat racing between 1970 and 1914, UK Book

g1632, **Winning Horseracing Handicapping**, Chuck Badone, £7.95pb, 120pp, Secrets of a successful horseracing handicapper, US Book

g1633, **RFO Racing Annual 2001**, Racing and Football Outlook, £4.95pb, 192pp, Contains 2000 Review, 2001 Review, Features, Race-courses and Betting Information, UK Book

g1634, **Timeform: Horses to Follow** - 2001 Flat season , Timeform, £5.95pb, 40pp, Timeform Horses to follow includes horses carefully cho-sen by members of Timeform's editorial staff from thousands with whose performance they are familiar. A selection of 10 is made for those who prefer a smaller list., UK Book

g1638, **Racing - Systems with the Pocket Calculator**, John White, £5.99pb, 96pp, This book can transform your chances of winning - with an ordinary pocket calculator. The logic of betting on horses and greyhounds is too often clouded by dubious tips and a heavy dependence on Lady Luck. Now put science to work for you by following some often startlingly successful methods of analysing form - so simple that a basic pocket cal-culator can give you your winner in seconds. Contains Which Races to Bet On, Evaluating the Odds, Selecting your Winner, Selecting your Winner., UK Book

g1640, **Horse-Racing's Strangest Races**, Andrew Ward, £8.99pb, 230pp, Extraordinary but true stories from over 150 years of racing, UK Book

g1641, **Horses in Training 2001**, Len Bell (Editor), £14.95pb, 816pp, 17, 000 horses, 641 trainers, jockeys' weights and retainers, UK Book

g1650, **Physicality Handicapping Made Easy**, Joe Takach, £19.95pb, pp, Takach Uses a form of handicapping based on what a person can ob-serve about the animals in a race. Factors that can eliminate a potentially poor performance or indicate a potentially good performance, which are covered here in detailed are: Walking Short, Ears and Their Significance in Betting Decisions; Do Tails Make a Difference; Muscling; Colour; En-ergy; Negative Equipment; Warm-ups and Warm-Downs; Profiting from Physicality Knowledge, US Manuscript

Apologies but the new edition of **Win at the Tote Placepot** has been de-layed...again!

LOTTERY

g1645, **Getting Lucky** - Answers to Nearly Every Lottery Question You Can Ask, Ben E Johnson, £6.95pb, 188pp, Everything you need to know about the big money games people play every day, US Book

g68, **Winning Lotto Everyday Players**, Prof Jones, £9.95pb, 138pp, Features strategies, explanations for strategies, tables and charts, wheeling systems and more, US Book

g652, **Basics Of Winning Lotto**, Prof Jones, £3.95pb, 56pp, Everything you need to know to play and win money at lotto and lottery games, US Book

g677, **National Lottery Book**, Sam Weren, £4.99pb, 126pp, Not as technical as Weren's other book but a lot of good tips and systems here for those who feel they aren't winning enough or regularly, UK Book

g710, **Playing Lotteries For Big Money**, Sam Weren, £12.95pb, 60pp, Excellent book for those wishing to take the lottery seriously. Covers: Basics of Bias, Frequency Analysis Skip and Hit Charts, Cluster Analysis, Wheeling, and lots more, UK Book

g886, **Winning Perms Lottery Jackpots**, Gwilym Roberts, £3pb, 12pp, Basic info for lottery Users, UK Book

g1148, **How To Win More**, Henze And Riedwyl, £15.95pb, 141pp, Designed to improve the return on your lottery investments. Improve your odds of winning larger amounts, US Book

g1227, **Living On The Lottery**, Hunter Davies, £4.99pb, 420pp, Follows 10 of the biggest winners for a year to see how their lives changed. Davies is always a good read, UK Book

g1228, **Everything About The Lotto**, E.Thompson, £7.99pb, 249pp, Everything you ever wanted to know about the lottery. Includes systems and strategies, US Book

g1229, **Regular Wins On National Lottery**, Dennis Jones, £3.99pb, 96pp, Jones is a retired bookmaker and has already had ten wins Using the system in this book, UK Book

g1230, **How To Win The Lottery**, Dr.M.Harding, £3.99pb, 53pp, Handy pocket guide includes: how the draw numbers behave, best ways of selecting numbers, methods to avoid pros and cons of syndicates, and pitfalls, UK Book g1360, **The Lottery**, Collins Gem, £4.99pb, 192pp, Is there any skill for the player? How much has been won and by whom? How do you organize a syndicate? What are the best numbers to pick? All these questions are answered in this handy pocket-sized book which is essential for anyone who ever buys a ticket. Many common myths are dispelled in this comprehensive book which captures the excitement of the lottery but also looks at the human interest, records, pitfalls and unusual facts have have arisen from a national institution. A chapter on the lottery and your stars will interest all who study numerology, astrology or just want to feel 'lucky', UK Book

g1389, **Lottery:** The Win that Tore a Family Apart, Rachel Halliwell, £5.99pb, 249pp, The true story of how the win of a lifetime tore a family apart, UK Book

g1394, **How to Win Lotteries**, Sweepstakes, and Contests in the 21st Century, Steve Ledoux , £14.95pb, 224pp, Steve Ledoux reveals the secrets that have earned him the title of American's Sweepstakes King, US Book

g1419, **It Could be You**: the Untold Story of the UK National Lottery, , £10.99pb, 270pp, This study reveals the politics, rivalries and tensions behind the winning of the licence and the running of the lottery. As the government prepares to renew the lottery licence, the authors pose some challenging questions. Was Camelot handed a licence to print money, as its critics suggest?, UK Book

g1438, **Lottery Syndicate Perm Package**, George Edmund Knowles , £4.99pb, Useful guide to help lottery winning, UK Book

g1472, **Official National Lottery Software Program**, £9.95, Ideal for all those who play the lottery. Packed with features it will do everything from helping you choose your numbers to automatically checking your numbers against each draw. If you manage a syndicate at home or work then the program can help here too. It will store all your different tickets, remind you when they need renewing and keep track of whether your group members have paid, UK software

g1475, **National Lottery Syndicate Agreement**, Law Pack, £4.99pb, pp, Set up and operate your own Syndicate and increase your chances of a Lucky Draw. Protect your prize money. Legally binding solicitor - approved. Valid throughout the UK, UK Pack

NFL AMERICAN FOOTBALL

g1288, **Pointspread Playbook 1999**, Al O'Donnell, £19.95pb, 104pp, In it's 21st year, this football gem is perfect to get your regular season angles and O/U research polished. Contains 3 years of spread and total records for every game, US Book

g1289, **How Pro Gamblers Beat the Pointspread**, J.R.Miller, £34.95pb, pp, American. One of the finest books for any level player, this takes the beginner through basics, then to the vig, standard deviation, reading the spread, pencilling in a prediction and more., US Book

g1294, **Complete Guide To Football Betting**, Feist & Sturgeon, £19.95pb, 306pp, American. Divided into 70 major sections this book is directed at the most significant points both beginners and experienced bettors need to understand., US Book

g1315, **1999 NFL Football Trend Notebook**, Bob Frederick, £29.95pb, 125pp, Contains over 200 trends for both sides and totals. Also includes 1999 schedule, pointspread record for the past 3 years showing record at home, away, favourite role, type of turf etc. , US Book

g1444, **Football Betting: Strategies for the Smart Player**, Kevin O'Neill , £24.95pb, 101pp, American football betting strategies for those who have decided to make a serious effort to become winning bettors., US spiral

POKER

g2, Winning Poker Serious Player, Edwin Silberstang, £12.95pb, 224pp, This 1992 book is introductory but structured for the player who wishes to attack the games with solid strategies while understanding the value of hidden pairs, positions and bluffing. US Book

g5, Holdem Poker, David Sklansky, £19.95pb, 110pp, The first definitive work on hold'em poker, still one of the most important and best selling. Primarily for newcomers but also contains sophisticated material for advanced players, Recommended, US Book

g26, Rules Of Neighbourhood Poker, Stewart Wolpin, £6.95pb, 345pp, Lots of different poker games not normally played in casinos. Also tips on the right food to serve (pizza) and the wrong food to serve (Chinese), US Book

g35, Poker Hold'em:Intermediate, Andy Nelson, £8.95pb, 72pp, Assumes the reader knows the basics. Covers playing position, practice 'reading opponents', studying the flop, interpreting what a raise means, knowing when to get out, US Book

g36, Hold'em Poker Advanced Players, Sklansky & Malmuth, £29.95pb, 212pp, Ideas discussed include: play on the first two cards, semi-bluffing, the free card, inducing bluffs, being beat on the river, staying with a draw etc, Recommended, US Book

g42, Poker: Omaha Book One, Andy Nelson, £8.95pb, 72pp, 7 chapters covering the basics: What Kind of Hands Win, Choosing a Starting Hand, Reading the Board, Investing in a Hand, Low Side Traps, Playing the Blinds, US Book

g49, A Friendly Game, Bert Morris, £17.95pb, 106pp, A book on how to protect yourself from cheats. Look out for tricks of the trade like tinted contact lenses, dealing 'seconds' and 'bottoms' and more, US Book

g88, Education Of A Poker Player, Herbert Yardley, £7.99pb, 160pp, This classic book is out on its own, not only as a poker playing manual but also as an exposure of the cynical reality behind the American dream. A marvellous autobiography about countless poker games and countless characters, about the railroad men, travelling salesmen, speculators, drunks, no hopers - even secret agents - whom Yardley saw through a tobacco haze across the green baize tables of the world, Available again Late 2001

g90, Gamblers, Grifters, Good Ol Boys, Bob Mason, £7.95pb, 175pp, Over forty short stories in this one, revealing the many facets of the gambling world, in the company of con men and horseplayers and many more., US Book

g93, **Poker: Omaha Hi/Lo Intermediate,** Andy Nelson, £8.95pb, 70pp, Includes: The Potential of the Flop, explaining why Hope is a Trap, the Art of Reading Players, Position Play, and Emotional Control, US Book

g96, **The Cincinnati Kid**, Richard Jessup, £4.99pb, pp, The classic book on which the Steve McQueen film was based. Has a different ending to the film and well worth a read. Nothing will replace McQueen though, UK Book — Limited stock

g108, **How To Play Winning Poker**, Avery Cardoza, £6.95pb, 90pp, For beginning to intermediate. How to recognise and play good cards, achieve maximum profits with winning hands, minimize losses on poor hands, how to Use pot odds etc, US Book

g129, **Wins, Places And Pros**, Tex Sheahan, £6.95pb, 144pp, A book of articles, covering strategy and stories about some of the great poker characters, US Book

g184, **Total Poker**, David Spanier, £6.99pb, 250pp, The 1977 book revised and updated, this covers the history, culture, technique and strategy of poker. The author visits the shop so signed copies are Usually available, Limited stock, UK Book

g239, **How to win at Stud Poker**, James Wickstead, £7.95pb, 156pp, Originally written in 1938 with a combination of mathematical flavour and with an eye toward the psychology of the game. About 5-card stud only, US Book

g314, **How To Win At Poker**, Reese and watkins, £6.95pb, 146pp, Covers jackpots, percentages, draw, lowball, draw with the bug, deuces wild, other variations of draw, 5-card stud, 7-card stud, and so on, US Book

g392, **Poker: Seven Card Stud**, Andy Nelson, £8.95pb, 67pp, Tells the novice how to protect himself, including the value of starting hands; how to sweep. Continues with proper moves on 4th, 5th, 6th and 7th streets. US Book

g429, **High-Low Split Poker Advanced**, Ray Zee, £34.95pb, 333pp, 7 card stud and Omaha 8 or better, for advanced players. Shows how a good eight-or-better high-low-split player can become a great eight-or-better player, US Book

g430, **The Theory Of Poker**, David Sklansky, £24.95pb, 276pp, The Theory of Poker puts you inside the heads of the greatest poker players. It tells you the all-important factors you should consider in a particular situation before determining what to do. It talks about the general theories and concepts of poker play that are operative in nearly every variation of poker and describes the thought processes of advanced players. Using sample hands, it analyses every aspect of a poker hand from the ante structure to play after the last card has been dealt in such games as five-card stud, seven-card stud, hold'em, draw lowball, and razz; or seven-card lowball. Also included for quick easy reference are an appendix of basic game rules and a glossary of poker terms. In short, a professional poker player teaches you how to think like one. Includes: bluffing and semi-bluffing, value of deception, the free card, slow playing, position, reading hands etc, Recommended, US Book

g445, **Seven Card Stud for Advanced Players**, Sklansky and Malmuth, £29.95pb, 219pp, Contains five major sections, but overall teaches a tight yet aggressive approach. Designed for medium limit games but suitable for advanced and regular players, US Book

g449, **Sklansky On Poker**, David Sklansky, £29.95pb, 181pp, A general overall advice book for the advanced player seeking to improve in hold em, draw, or razz. There are 85 pages solely on the latter. Rest covers general concepts, US Book

g450, **Poker Essays**, Malmuth & Sklansky, £24.95pb, 262pp, Lots of ideas packed into this for the serious player. Topics covered include: general concepts, technical ideas, image, tournament notes, poker quizzes, and much more advice besides, US Book

g465, **Supersystem**, Doyle Brunson, £50pb, 604pp, Considered to be one of the best books on poker ever. Mandatory reading for anyone planning to enter a major tournament or play no-limit, The classic must have book, US Book

g489, **Poker Hold'em Book One**, Andy Nelson, £8.95pb, 74pp, 7 chapters for the beginner: the Basics, Starting Hands, Position, Patience, the Blinds, What Hands Win, and the Danger of Copying Bad Players, US Book

g499, **Poker: Seven Ways To Win**, Andy Nelson, £8.95pb, 68pp, The seven chapters are: Patience, More On Patience, Position Has Power, Don't Play Rags, Coping With A Bad Beat, A Contingency Plan For A Losing Streak, Staying One Card Too Long, US Book

g505, **Basics Of Winning Poker**, J Edward Allen, £3.95pb, 59pp, Handbook for the beginner, covering the rules and its variations, how to bet, which hands to play etc, US Book

g506, **Fundamentals Of Poker**, Mason Malmuth, £5.95pb, 70pp, Slim handbook for seven-card stud and Texas hold-em plus insights into winning at Omaha, razz, and lowball., US Book g522, **Foolproof**, Richard Allen, £49.95pb, 222pp, 2 vols. U.S. a training program with materials that include the textbook (146 pages) a workbook (76 pages) and a starting hand guide you can Use as you play, US Book

g601, **Winning Concepts In Draw & Lowball**, Mason Malmuth, £24.95pb, 378pp, For the typical player and the pro. Text is partitioned into sections that are designed to help all players grow and improve, US Book

g624, **Omaha Holdem Poker**, Bob Ciaffone, £15pb, 106pp, New edition, 30 pages longer. Covers rules, basics, betting procedures, importance of being suited, evaluating starting hands, pot limit play, percentages, Hi-lo split, tournament strategy, US Book

g629, **More Hold'em Excellence**, Lou Krieger, £24.95pb, 221pp, 27 sections in this one for the advanced player including Early, Middle and Late Position, Betting the Farm, The Right Seat, Aggression, Image, etc, US Book

g638, **Poker Tournament Tips From Pros**, Shane Smith, £19.95pb, 101pp, Should help you win low stakes limit tournaments. Tells how to vary your play in four stages of tournaments: opening, middle, late and final table, US Book

g663, **Johnny Moss: Poker's Finest**.., Don Jenkins, £8.95pb, 214pp, The authorised biography of one of the great poker players of all time. He wons millions and lost millions, a skinny kid who never made it to third grade who beat the lot, US Book

g664, **Playpoker, Quit Work, Sleep Till Noon**, John Fox, £14.95pb, 343pp, This is solely on draw poker and deals with nearly every aspect of play. Has mathematical tables, and dozens of psychological ploys. Great title too. US Book

g666, **Caros Fundamental Poker Secrets**, Mike Caro, £9.95pb, 150pp, Tells and psychology; tournament advice; playing five card draw, seven stud or hold'em. When to raise, fold, call, bluff projecting the right image etc., US Book

g791, **Winning Low Limit Hold'em**, Lee Jones, £24.95pb, 176pp, Revised 2nd edition of this popular book. Written for the beginner or someone wanting to improve his skills. Emphasis on tight but aggressive play, and sections on the mechanics of the game, Recommended, US Book

g800, **Poker: 101 Ways To Win**, Andy Nelson, £17.95pb, 224pp, Includes: learning to be a winner, the power of position, starting hands, combat preparation, reading opponents, coping with a check raise and more, US Book g827, **Tournament Poker,** Tom McEvoy, £34.95pb, 344pp, Expensive but essential for the serious player. 20 chapters cover some of the most vital areas. Also how to maintain emotional stability, partnerships, toking, working a deal at the final table, US Book

g829, **Seven Card Stud Hi/Lo Split 8s**, Andy Nelson, £8.95pb, 67pp, Based on 8 or better for the low side, book provides 6 chapters covering how to go for high, low only, or how to try to 'sweep the table' and get it all, US Book

g830, **Poker: Seven More Ways To Win**, Andy Nelson, £8.95pb, 70pp, Includes: preparing for the game, comparisons between good and bad strategy, table image, how to avoid hands that can sting, getting maximum returns for good hands., US Book

g841, **Winners Guide Texas Hold'em Poker**, Ken Warren, £14.95pb, 210pp, An excellent book for beginners. 14 chapters look at the basics and seven pages have hold em odds and also charts and tables. Warren shows you how to become a confident, proficient winner in home, club and casino games, and how to play every hand from every position with every type of flop. You'll discover winning concepts found nowhere else. Includes the most complete chapter on Hold'em odds in print. So they say, Recommended, US Book

g865, **Thursday-Night Poker**, Peter O Steiner, £16pb, 426pp, For the serious weekly-to-monthly player, this has illustrated, in-depth discussions of nearly 50 hands, and chapters on 5-card, 7-card, Omaha, Hi-Lo, and others, US Book

g866, **Handbook Of Winning Poker**, Edwin Silberstang, £9.95pb, 160pp, An easy to read guide to more than 10 popular poker varieties. For beginners and intermediates, US Book

g884, **7 Card Stud:** Win Med/Low Limits, Roy West, £24.95pb, 156pp, Includes: the Rule of Two, stealing the antes, getting knowledge on your opponents, remembering exposed cards, reading the board, outsmarting in shorthanded games and more, US Book

g889, **Omaha Hi-Lo Poker (8 Or Better)**, Shane Smith, £16.95pb, 82pp, For beginners and middle-level players who have a basic knowledge of the game of Omaha Hi-Lo but wish to improve their skills, US Book

g890, **Low-Limit Casino Poker**, Shane Smith, £5pb, 31pp, Six chapters discusses 'divers', surviving, seven-card stud, hold 'em, Omaha high/low, 8 or better, and tournaments, US Book

g897, **Unsinkable Titanic Thompson**, Carlton Stowers, £14.95pb, 234pp, Biography of one of the most flamboyant gamblers and hustlers of the century. Real name Alvin Clarence Thomas, he died in 1974 aged 82. One of the gambling legends, US Book

g901, **Poker: A Winners Guide,** Andy Nelson, £10.95pb, 212pp, This teaches everything you need to know from the basics to the finer points of the game. Nelson teaches classes on poker and has written several other books too, US Book

g927, **Poker Hold'em Advanced**, Andy Nelson, £8.95pb, 71pp, Five chapters for players familiar with Hold Em. Emotional Control, Playing the Cards, Playing the Players, Tools of the Trade, Creative Fixing., US Book

g961, **John Patricks Casino Poker,** John Patrick, £16.95pb, 206pp, In casino poker the odds are the same as in poker played at home; the only difference is the house cut, which ranges from 5 percent of a pot to a fixed maximum. For intermediates, Not recommended, US Book

g964, **Poker, Gaming And Life**, David Sklansky, £24.95pb, 207pp, A collection of articles that have appeared in various publications. Most are about poker or gambling, US Book

g965, **Gambling For A Living**, Sklansky & Malmuth, £24.95pb, 304pp, Covers blackjack, horse racing, poker, slots, and most other things and gives good advice for those wanting to become a professional gambler, US Book

g1028, **Pot-Limit And No-Limit Poker**, Reuben & Ciaffone, £15pb, 218pp, Explains the proper concepts and strategies Used for playing pot-limit and no-limit poker. Includes hold'em, Omaha, 7 card stud, and several varieties of lowball., US Book

g1070, **Championship No/Pot Limit Hold Em**, T J Clouthier, £34.95pb, 209pp, Expensive but sells well. Advice involves five chapters which try to prepare you for crucial tournament decisions. Co-written with Tom McEvoy, Recommended, US Book

g1072, **Shut Up and Deal**, Jesse May, £6.99pb, 215pp, Excellent first novel by young American writer ,poker player, and Channel 4 commentator, which has been described as the best gambling novel since Mario Puzo's 'Fools Die'. Cool, hip, and why haven't you read it yet? , UK Book

g1084, **Championship Stud**, Stern & Johnson, £34.95pb, 202pp, Five chapters outline winning concepts for medium- limit cash games and stage by stage strategies for winning major tournaments. Chapter 6 is general tournament strategy, US Book

g1085, **Poker Talk**, Michael Weisenberg, £14.95pb, 186pp, From A-Z, a complete reference on the colourful and secretive language of poker.

Helpful for home games, card rooms or casinos, or those researching the subject, US Book

g1087, **Mike Caros Guide To SuperSystem**, Mike Caro, £19.95pb, 86pp, A fresh insight into the Bible of all poker books, hat help you understand Brunson's original 1978 book, US Book

g1108, **Poker Tournament Strategies,** Sylvester Suzuki, £19.95pb, 181pp, Poker tournaments are very different from normal poker games, and very few excel at both. Suzuki tells how you can. Especially good on smaller rebuy tournaments, US Book

g1136, **P$Ychology Of Poker P$Ymplified**, David R.Whalen, £24.95pb, 158pp, For intermediates. 18 chapters emphasizing the ability to observe, evaluate and remember player moves, US Book

g1169, **Rounders,** Kevin Canty, £5.99pb, 194pp, Mike McDermott is a master card-player, at large in New York's underground world of high-stakes poker games. Mike tries to control his obsession with gambling by focussing on his studies at law school, but when his childhood friend Worm is released from prison, Mike is inexorably drawn back to the world of Rounders as he is forced to protect Worm from the violence his friend has unwittingly unleashed, UK Book

g1193, **Poker Essays 2,** Mason Malmuth, £24.95pb, 286pp, This includes essays on General Concepts, Technical Ideas, Structure, Strategic Ideas, In the Cardrooms, Quizzes, Erroneous Concepts and more. For serious players. , US Book

g1194, **Poker Expertise Thru Probability**, Robert Riley, £34.95pb, 186pp, For the poker player who doesn't have a clue about figuring odds and probabilities. Riley taught probability to high school students, so he is easy to follow, US Book

g1195, **Poker Tournament Tactics**, D.R.Sherer, £24.95pb, 171pp, How to get the tournament money, how to approach rebuys strategically, how the curve affects strategy, playing against short and tall stacks, bluffing, and making deals at final table, US Book

g1196, **Pokerfarce And Pokertruth**, Ray Michael B, £19.95pb, 246pp, In this you'll be taken to a serious game and be sitting beside the author. You'll be a spectator to the drama of poker, meet the players close-up, see their strengths and weaknesses, US Book

g1209, **No Fold Em, Hold Em,** D.R.Sherer, £19.95pb, 110pp, How to win with little cards in medium and low limit hold em with some of the sneakiest logic you'll ever find in a poker book, US Book

g1210, **Improve Your Poker**, Bob Ciaffone, £20pb, 220pp, This covers beating a loose game and tight/loose play, deception and bluffing, the mental side, reading opponents, 6 pages on Omaha, overbetting, position, plus more, US Book

g1211, **Hold Em Odds Book**, Mike Petriv, £24.95pb, 207pp, A primer on calculating hold em odds for the layman. Illustrated, packed with charts, tables and mathematics. No other work is devoted purely to this subject, Recommended, US Book

g1212, **Official Rules And Regulations** Manual, Ron Cramer, £9.95pb, 74pp, Tries to create a standardised set of rules for the benefit of the house and the player. Cover general rules, dealing, ranking of suits, terms, button procedures, stud, draw, kill games, and Chinese poker, US Book

g1220, **Championship Omaha**, T.J.Cloutier, £34.95pb, 230pp, Discusses the differences and similarities of the 3 versions of Omaha, then moves into detailed strategies for each game. For advanced players, US Book

g1224, **Winning Poker Systems,** Norman Zadeh, £10pb, 208pp, Back in print, this 1974 title is still worth a look because of its charts, tables, and mathematical work, from a brilliant theorist. Covers draw, lowball, 5, 6, and 7 card hi lo and split. Nothing on Hold em, US Book

g1256, **Seven Card Stud Poker**, K.Othmer, £25pb, 257pp, Othmer Uses charts and clear explanations to show the anatomy of 7 stud hands. Serious stud players can Use these insights to destroy those not in the know., US Book

g1257, **Hold Em Excellence**, Lou Krieger, £19.95pb, 159pp, 18 chapters cover the most important factors a beginner must master to earn a profit. Indexed and illustrated, US Book

g1268, **Where Did It All Go Right?,** Al Alvarez, £25hb, 320pp, Long awaited memoirs of the author of The Biggest Game In Town. Covers all his hobbies including poker, mountaineering, and flying, UK Book

g1296, **Gentleman Gambler**, Johnny Hale, £14.95pb, 227pp, Autobiography of famous poker player who has played with the likes of Moss, Binion, and Straus. US Book

g1299, **Real Poker**, The Cooke Collection, Roy Cooke, £19.95pb, 400pp, This is five years of Cooke's columns from Card Player magazine. A wide range of advice for advanced players, US Book

g1300, **Little Book Of Poker**, David Spanier, £4.99pb, 170pp, A collection of Spanier's entertaining articles from the Independent. An excellent browzing book full of anecdotes and general poker wisdom. UK Book g1314, **101 Tournament Hands**, D.R.Sherer, £17.95sp, 150pp, A manual with pictorials of tournament hands for hold'em, Omaha, and 7 stud, saying how the author would play each of them, US Book

g1331, **Zen And The Art Of Po**ker, Larry W. Phillips, £8.99pb, 175pp, You can master the art of poker with this quintessential guide that shows you how to apply the philosophies of Zen so you can play your best game, every game. Written by a professional poker player this gives you the edge you need as it delivers winning strategies on everything from getting in the zone to playing on instinct. You'll learn to master: The one hundred essential rules of the game. The Zen of lying low... and playing tight. Trends in your luck cycles, US Book

g1358, **Championship Hold 'Em**, Cloutier & Mcevoy, £34.95pb, 319pp, Inside information on limit-hold'em tournament strategies that have led the authors to numerous final tables - plus 20 illustrated hands with play-by-ply analysis for various situations, US Book

g1370, **Ms Poker: Up Close & Personal**, Susie Isaacs, £22pb, 246pp, This book is different from most of the poker books you'll find because it mixes humour and human interest as well as poker tournament strategy. You will be entertained as you learn the story of Susie Isaacs, US Book

g1374, **Life is a Game of Poker**, Jim Chilters, £15pb, 103pp, Poker fiction, US Book

g1375, **Playing Low Limit Hold'em**: The 20-4-50 Way, Bob Turgeon, £10.95pb, 91pp, Can make you a Steady Winner in Low Limit Games, US Book

g1409, **Poker for Dummies**, , £13.99pb, 298pp, Step-by-step guide on how to bet, bluff, and play your way to the top, from seven-card stud and high-low splits to Omaha and Texas Hold'em, US Book

g1424, **Secrets of Winning Video Poker**, Avery Cardoza , £14.95pb, 168pp, Video poker can be beat - with the odds - but only if you follow the winning strategies shown here. All strategies are based on exact probability calculations and simplified with a negligible loss so that anyone can have fun whil playing, US Book

g1434, **The Psychology of Poker**, Alan N. Schoonmaker, £24.95pb, 330pp, Includes; The Right Stuff, The Right Skills, Styles and Ratings, The Loose-Aggressive Player, The Loose-Passive Player, The Tight-Passive Player, The Tight-Aggressive Player, Our Deadly Sins, US Book

g1435, **Inside the Poker Mind**: Essays on Hold'em and General Poker Concepts, John Feeney , £24.95pb, 275pp, Topics Include: Playing Too Many Hands, Self-Weighting Cold Calls, Short-Handed Play: Don't Miss Out, The Strategic Moment in Hold'em, Countering a Good Reader, A

Poker Player in Therapy, Thought on the Effects of the Poker Literature, US Book

g1496, **Poker Strategy**: Proven Principles for Winning Play, A D Livingston, £14.95pb, 224pp, Beginning with the principles of and strategies behind the game, Livingston goes on to explain poker's often intricate mathematics, and includes handy odds tables to guide the reader. Also covered are dozens of poker variations, from Anaconda to Zig-Zag. US Book

g1497, Winner's Guide to Casino Poker, Edwin Silberstang, £5.99pb, 310pp, This comprehensive poker guide gives you an expert's look at: Representative hands, including step-by-step advice, all the popular casino pker games, including Texas Hold'em, Seven-Card Stud and Hi-Lo variations, Betting strategies, the art of bluffing, and how to size up other players' strategies, how to establish- and manage-your backroll, US Book

g1500, **Winning a Living**, Texas Bill, £19.95sp, 151pp, The professional's guide to Poker Profits featuring winning strategies for Hold'em, Omaha, Omaha Hi-Lo, Seven Card Stud, Razz and tournament play, US Book

g1503, **Poker Odds**, Frank R. Wallace, £0.6pb, 17pp, Reprinted from the Advanced Concepts of Poker. This booklet compiles the following card odds: Rank of hands, Pat Hand Odds, Draw Odds, Stud Odds, Lowball Odds and Wild Card Odds, US Book

g1504, **Awesome Profits**, George Elias, £29.95pb, 383pp, Everything you need to know to improve your wins in home games or casinos is covered. 7-Card Stud, 7- Card Hi-Lo Stud, Omaha Hi-Lo, Lo-Ball, Razz, Omaha, Texas Hold'em, Pineapple plus 11 homes games. US Book

g1505, **Official Dictionary of Poker**, Michael Wiesenberg, £14.95pb, 277pp, This completely updated and revised Mike Caro University edition contains the entire spectrum of poker terminology, from common to the obscure, illustrated by thousands of examples actually heard in cardrooms, US Book

g1506, **Omaha Poker in a Nutshell,** J.C. Moore, £14.95pb, 38pp, A Totally Concept for Low-Limit Omaha Poker Hi and Hi-Lo Combined. No guesswork for Starting and Straying Hands all you need to do is count, US Book

g1508, **Caribbean Stud Poker & Let it Ride**, J.Phillip Vogel, £15.95pb, 200pp, Learn all of the secrets and strategies the professionals Use to beat the casinos. With 200 pages of easy-to-read charts, tables and explanations, US Book g1509, **Winning Caribbean Stud Poker and Let It Ride**, Avery Cardoza, £9.95pb, 168pp, This fun and informative book is an easy-to-read and complete guide to winning at Caribbean Stud Poker and Let It Ride. From the rules of the games and the basics of play, to money management, and the basic and advanced winning strategies, US Book

g1510, **How to Play Poker and Win,** Brian McNally, £7.99pb, 156pp, Produced by the professional poker-playing team behind Late Night Poker, UK Book

g1517, **Texas Hold'em Poker**: McNally's Guidelines to the Universal Rules and Procedures of Poker, McNally, £5pb, 36pp, Compiles guidelines for players not familiar with the rules, prodcedure and etiquette and to encourage existing players to reach a better standard of conduct at the table, UK Book

g1518, **The Hand I Played**: A Poker Memoir, David Spanier, £16.99hb, 246pp, The acclaimed gambling writer and journalist David Spanier looks back at his life-long love of poker in this compelling and fascinating memoir, UK Book

g1521, **Optimal Strategy for Pai Gow Poker**, Stanford Wong, £14.95pb, 160pp, Topics include getting an edge, optimal strategy, approximate strategy, and miscellaneous details, US Book

g1545, **Caro's Book of Tells** - The Body Language of Poker, Mike Caro, £24.95pb, 352pp, The long awaited revised edition of Mike Caro's tells book. This manual contains over 170 photo-illustrations showing the actual tells that you can Use to destroy your friends or Use in poker rooms. You'll learn how to spot and understand subtle shrugs, sighs, shaking hands, misdirected bets, and much more. You'll understand humming, tapping fingers, bored stares, and every meaningful trait your poker opponents display - whether they're acting or unaware. This new millennium edition adds some play-by-play examples, new concepts, artistically rendered illustrations . Also marvel at some of the poorest dress sense featured in a 21st century book, Recommended, US Book

g1546, **Caro's Major Poker Seminar**, Mike Caro, £24.95 video, 60 minutes video, Self-proclaimed Mad Genius Mike Caro present this entertaining and informative video based on the inaugural class at Mike Caro University of Poker held at Hollywood Park. The presentation is based on many of the aspects portrayed in his books and will help improve your poker with each viewing, US Video

g1547, **Pro Poker Tells,** Mike Caro, £59.95 video, 90 minutes video, Revealing the secrets of professional poker. Mike Caro was the first to seriously study poker tells and here is an important additional to any poker players armoury. In a two volume set and concentrating on reading opponents - recognising tells that indicate that they have strong or weak hands. Also helps players recognise that they too have tells which are giving away strong hands, US Video

g1548, **Annual World Series of Poker** (19th, 20th, 21st), £39.95, 90 minutes video, Highlights of the 1988, 1989, 1990 of the annual Binion's Hotel and casino Poker Tournament with play-by-play analysis, US Video

g1549, **22nd Annual (1991 Finals),** £25.95, 45 minutes video, Watch how Brad Daugherty won $1 million on how Tucson Don won $402, 000 by finishing second, US Video

g1550, **23rd Annual (1992 Finals),** £25.95, 45 minutes video video, Hamid Dastmalchi prevailed in this one which included one big pot for more than a million dollars from second-place finisher Tom Jacobs of Denver, US Video

g1551, **24th Annual (1993 Finals),** £14.95, 70 minutes video, Shows the excitement of the final won by Jim Bechtel, US Video

g1552, **25th Annual (1994) Finals**, £14.95, 45 minutes video, A tournament that featured the first-ever straight flush in the history of the series in its Silver Anniversary. Russ Hamilton is the victor beating Hugo Vincent after nine hours of play, US Video

g1553, **26th Annual (1995) Finals**, £14.95 , 45 minutes video, Ring-game specialist Dan Harrington transfers his skills to pocket the million-dollar prize, US Video

g1554, **28th Annual (1997) Finals**, £14.95 , 45 minutes video, 25 year old Huck Seed wins the wonga, US Video

g1556, **29th Annual (1998) Finals,** £14.95 , 45 minutes video, Thuan Scotty Nguyen wins, Kevin McBride second with TJ Cloutier coming in third, US Video

g1557, **30th Annual (1999)** Finals, £14.95, 45 minutes video, Irish invader Noel Furlong wins with a famous last hand, US Video

g1561, **Caro Power Poker Seminar**, Mike Caro, £39.95 , 60 minutes video, The self-proclaimed mad genius offers advice on how to improve play using strategy, psychology and statistics, along with his speciality tells, US Video

g1569, **Maverick's Guide to Poker**, £5.95pb, 169pp, Tie in with the film starring Mel Gibson - despite this it is a handy reference book including How to Play Draw, How to Play 5-Card Stud, Seven-Card Stud: The Double Action Game, Hold'em: The Gambler's Game, High-Low Stud: Call of the Wild, Deadly Mathematics of Poker, US Book g1584, **Serious Poker**, Dan Kimberg, £12.95pb, 318pp, Basic Rules and Strategy Record Keeping Money Management Tournaments Expectation and Variance Poker Math Common Fallacies The Language of Poker, US Book

g1586, **Percentage Hold'em** - The book of Numbers, Justin Case, £35sp, 233pp, Not a basic how to play book. This book contains more than a hundred pages of charts and tables, an intense computer analysis of the precise odds on any hand, in any game, derived from the play of 929, 000, 000 hands. This is the Book of Numbers for Texas Hold'em. This book is for the Percentage Player, who already knows it is possible to play any game based upon probabilities, US Book

g1588, **1999 Tournament of Champions of Poker**, , £19.95 , 60 minutes video, Competition between some of the world greatest players at Orleans casino in Vegas, David Chiu was crowned champion of champions, US Video

g1604, **Video Poker - Optimum Play**, Dan Paymar, £19.95pb, 199pp, This book will show you: Why certain video poker machines offer the highest potential payback of any games in the casinos, How to recognise games that offer 100% payback, How to avoid the deceptive short-pay machines, How big a bankroll you will need in order to have any desired chance of hitting a jackpot and most importantly Precision Play - how to quickly and easily make the optimum draw to maximise your win rate - without having to memorise long tables, US Book

g1605, **Video Poker for the Winner**, Marten Jensen , £9.95pb, 208pp, Jensen not only shows you Video Poker machines that will give you an actual advantage over the house but the actual percentages and best strategies to beat every popular machine played today!, US Book

g1606, **Video Poker Answer Book** - How to Attack Variation in a Casino Favourite, John Grochowski, £12.95pb, 277pp, Gives his easy-to-understand insights into how the machines work and the best strategies for attacking up-to-date variations on this casino standard. How does the player recognise a high-paying machine? Does the method of play change on new machines that have the customer play three, four, five, 10 or even 50 hands at once?, US Book

g1610, **Omaha Split 8 or Better for Low**, John Payne, £18pb, 64pp, Valuable advice for this game divided into eight sections including Basic Structure, Starting Hands, The Low Factor, The Straight Factor, The FlUSh Factor, Trips, Full Houses, Quads, US Book

g1619, **Scarne's Guide to Modern Poker**, John Scarne, £14pb, 307pp, Scarne lays down the rules of all 117 forms of poker - including the latest variations. In this bet you will learn to bet like an expert, protect yourself from poker cheats, Use probabilities to enhance your game, balance caution against betting courage, bluff successfully, master the 20 vital strategies every expert player must know, US Book

g1623, **Bicycle Playing Cards (Blue),** £2.99, Bicycle Playing Cards - N.B Postage will be charged at £0.50 for UK customers, Playing Cards

g1624, **Bicycle Playing Cards (Red),** £2.99, Bicycle Playing Cards - N.B Postage will be charged at £0.50 for UK customers, Playing Cards

NB—we have other types of playing cards available at various times— phone Scott on 020 74330 1021 or check the website

g1626, **Poker: Bets, Bluffs, and Bad Beats,** A. Alvarez, £20hb, 128pp, Acclaimed author and poker insider Al Alvarez (The Biggest Game in Town, Where Did it All Go Right?) celebrates the evolution of the pastime that has tested the characters of penny-ante players and High-Stakes gamblers the world over. Combining lively text with over 100 evocative colour and black-and-white images. , UK Book

g1647, **The Greatest Book for Winners!,** George Epstein, £24.95pb, 296pp, The four basic rules for strategies for winning at the game of poker - seven card stud and Texas Hold'em, US Book

g1648, **Texas Hold'em Poker: Claiming $2 - $5,** G Conly, £32pb, Includes Audio CD Extra. Begin to Win!, US Book

NEW POKER SOFTWARE

We have now added the popular Wilson Software to our stock

g1668, **Turbo Texas Hold'Em for Windows** – Version 4.0 – Wilson Software, £69.00, The new updated version includes Test your Hold'em skill by challenging the best computer player. Advice as you play: 20 different sets of strategies before the flop. Computer player toughened up and made more realistic. Unlimited raising when heada-up. Much more control over the computer players' toughness settings. These new features have been added to this popular software supplied on CD whilst maintaining the enhanced features from over versions

g1669, **Tournament Texas Hold'Em for Windows** – Version 2.0 – Wilson Software, £49.00, Features include: Choice of limit, no-limit or Pot-limit play. Control of tournament size. Play in a single table satellite tournament with 10 players up to a 100 table tournament with over 900 entrants. 2001 World Series of Poker final format is included. Play a complete tournament or jump to the final table

g1670, **Turbo 7- Card Stud for Windows** – Version 3 – Wilson Software, £69.00, New features added include: Test your stud skill by challenging the best computer player. Rake Option to drag the pot during play. Expanded play logic for low pairs. Dead card buttons which shows all of your dead cards. Pop-up tips with helpful info about the game. Option to just deal calling hands. Option to just deal raising hands. Improved advisor. Tougher computer players

The final software is available to order – please allow 21 days for delivery

g1671, **Turbo Omaha High-Low Split for Windows** – Wilson Software, £69.00, Recommended for all those who wish to make Omaha High-Low their main game

g1672, **Turbo Omaha High Only for Windows** – Wilson Software, £69.00, Software which enables all Omaha High players to sharpen their skills

g1673, **Turbo Stud – 8 or Better for Windows** – Wilson Software, £69.00, A great game and a great tool for people who want to improve their Stud 8/or better game

ROULETTE

g29, Thirteen Against The Bank, Norman Leigh, £6.99pb, 203pp, The story of the man who broke the bank at the roulette table with an unbeatable system. This all took place in 1966 in Nice and tells you how the system works. A classic, Recommended, UK Book

g177, The Newtonian Casino, Thomas Bass, £8.99pb, 329pp, A team of physicists and computer whizz-kids build a computer that predicts the motion of a roulette wheel, fit it in the sole of a shoe and wreak casino chaos!, UK Book

g427, Basic Roulette, Bert Walker, £4.95pb, 79pp, This primer advises the novice on the fundamental rules and methods of play. Geared to the U.S, US Book

g441, Basics Of Winning Roulette, J Edward Allen, £3.95pb, 58pp, A small handbook covering the rules and variations, the bets available, the payoffs, the odds, and inside secrets and strategies, US Book

g531, Beating The Wheel, Russell T Barnhart, £14.95pb, 208pp, This mainly concerns biased wheels, and a unique system based on escalating small bets. Written by an expert who has been winning for over thirty years, US Book

g876, John Patricks Roulette, John Patrick, £16.95pb, 257pp, For the player seeking ideas and angles. Covers streak play, money management, crooked wheels, crooked dealers, several betting methods and much more, US Book

g957, Beat The Casino At Roulette, Professor Garland, £12.95pb, 110pp, Explains the difference between the U.S. and European wheels. Presents a 'staking system' that allows you to keep track of what you've bet already, & then continue, US Book

g980, Spin Roulette Gold, Frank Scoblete, £14.95pb, 223pp, Covers such topics as biased wheels, big number and sector slicing strategies, and the chameleon strategy, plus 10000 actual spins on roulette wheels to test your systems against, US Book

g982, Playing Roulette As A Business, R.J.Smart, £12.95pb, 165pp, Now back in print, this is written by a Nevada croupier who instructs players how to play 'corners' and profit nearly 90% of the time, US Book

g1004, Secrets Of Winning Roulette, Martin Jensen, £12.95pb, 201pp, Everything you need to know, including biased wheels, betting systems, ball control and prediction, protecting against getting cheated etc. American, like all these roulette books, US Book

g1134, **Signature Bets**, Marcia Mcdowell, £19.95pb, 66pp, One of the first surveillance books ever to detail what the House is looking for when it suspects a player has found a Biased Wheel. Illustrated, US Book

g1135, **Roulette System Test**er, £24.95pb, 299pp, Contains 15,000 actual spins in multiple formats. Includes distribution and deviation charts on inside numbers. All decisions recorded in an unnamed Vegas casino, US Book

g1137, **Roulette For Weekend Gambler**, J.R.Miller, £9.95pb, 72pp, Includes more than half a dozen betting systems and how to Use them, also How to Spot Really Bad Betting Systems., US Book

g1251, **Roulette 20,000 Spins**, £5pb, pp, 20,000 actual spins from casino at Macao. Single zero, UK Book

g1573, **Roulette Recorder Single 0**, £2.50pb, 22pp, Wallet sized book designed to record the roulette numbers that appear during the night. Photocopiable, US Book

g1574, **Roulette Recorder**, £2.50pb, 22pp, Wallet sized book designed to record the roulette numbers that appear during the night. Photocopiable, US Book

g1583, **Roulette Eurotester** - 100,000+ Actual Casino Single Zero Numbers, Erick St Germain, £22pb, 180pp, Actual Spins from a Major European Casino. Over 100, 000 Single Zero Roulette Decisions. The smart and economical way to develop a winning strategy, US Book

g1627, **Roulette for Fun and Profit**, Arthur John Bourner, £8.99pb, 217pp, This is an intelligent players' guide to carefully tried and tested method of play that will challenge conventional thinking about the game and surprise you. It is formulated and written with the same clarity that infUses the argument by a professional accountant. Novice or experienced player, you will benefit by this book; a revolutionary system with quiet confidence, UK Book

SOCCER (or real Football as we like to call it)

g6, Football Pools, Scientific Analysis, Frank George, £10.95pb, 108pp, Includes chapters on Strategies for Pools Forecasting, Staking Methods, and Strategies in Action., UK Book

g457, Win Fixed Odds Football Betting, Malcolm Boyle, £2.99pb, 277pp, This is the 93/94 edition, but was the first book to deal with the subject of fixed odds. Was 6.99 but now 2.99, UK Book

g756, Winning The Pools, Dennis Jones, £4.99pb, 138pp, Professional pools analyst Jones lets you in on his tips, tricks, and truths about the addictive weekly gamble, UK Book

g903, Football Fortunes, Bill Hunter, £6.99pb, 150pp, Results, forecasting, gambling and computing. Covers fundamentals of results predictions, laws of probabilities and odds, detailed explanations of forecasting systems and staking strategies., UK Book

g1274, RFO Football Annual. 1999/2000, RFO, £3.95pb, 192pp, Pocket guide to the coming season with stats from last season and all this seasons fixtures. Introduction by John Motson and a few other articles too., UK Book

g1383, Gambling on Goals: A Century of Football Betting, Graham Sharpe, £15.99pb, 240pp, History of 125 years of football betting., UK Book

g1425, The Essential Football Betting Guide, Paul Steele, £15pb, 231pp, Learn all about the football coupon. Find out what the odds mean and how to compile them yourself. Predict the winners of the divisions and cups in August. Find out if the Ante-Post odds are value. See the results of systems thoroughly tested to see which is best. Learn how to find the Penetration values of each team. Find out when and by whom the goals are scored. These are just some of the topics covered in this excellent book, copies of which are now very limited, UK Book

g1459, Rothmans Football Yearbook 2000-2001, edited Glenda Rollin and Jack Rollin , £18.99pb, 976pp, 31st edition of the sport's leading authority includes, Invaluable players' directory, Complete Euro 2000 round-up: results, teams, scorers, goal times, crowds, Fully comprehensive match-by-match guide to English and Scottish League and Cup games, Review of the major European cup competitions, English, Scottish and international fixtures for 2000-2001, UK Book

g1514, Football Betting to Win: Speculating on the Beautiful Game, Jacques Black, £9.99pb, 224pp, A brand new, completely up to date book on all aspects of football betting from the Pools to Fixed Odds and the huge growth in football spread betting, UK Book

g1528, **Tales from the Boot Camps**, Steve Claridge, £7.99pb, 267pp, Charts both the highs and lows of Claridge's career - from training sessions on dog-fouled parks at Aldershot to the last-minute in a Wembley Final; from a successful season in the top flight with Leicester to life at Fratton Park, where Steve Claridge is still making newspaper headlines. Claridge also talks frankly about his addiction to gambling, UK Book

g1572, **How to Win the Pools**, Arthur James, £3.99pb, 128pp, Provides 30 well-tested ways that might bring you a close closer winning the pools - strangely doesn't come with a guarantee, UK Book

GAMBLING SOFTWARE

g1170, **Video Poker Strategy**, Computer Game, £20, CD ROM for Windows. Complete strategies for over 60 of the most readily found high-return poker machines of the U.S. Multimedia sounds and full motion video., US software

g1171, **World Series Of Poker**, De Luxe Pak, Computer Game, £20, CD ROM for Windows. US. This has 16 casino games in it, from blackjack, roulette, keno, craps, slots, baccarat, and also the original World Series of Poker, which Used to be on a separate disk. Excellent value., US software

g1172, **Masque Blackjack**, Computer Game, £15, CD ROM for Windows and DOS. Four complete strategies by Julian Braun, encompassing basic and advanced play for single and multiple decks., US software

g1173, **Caribbean Stud Poker**, Computer Game, £15, CD ROM for Windows. Interactive tutorial, it teaches the tutor what to hold, when to fold, and what to expect while playing. Includes on-line video film footage., US software

g1181, **5-Game Super Pak**, Computer Game, £15, CD ROM for windows. Five of the most popular games ever put on computer. Includes Solitaire Antics, Casino Video Poker, Casino Blackjack, Casino Caribbean Stud Poker, and Chess Net 3., US software

See section on New Arrived Poker software at the end of Poker

SPORTS BETTING

g594, **Caesars Palace Book Sports Betting**, Bert Sugar, £14.95pb, 186pp, Covers football, basketball, baseball, hockey and boxing. Defines betting terms and numbers, tells what factors to look for in each sport., US Book

g960, **John Patricks Sports Betting**, John Patrick, £16.95pb, 307pp, This covers bankroll, money management, knowledge of the game, and discipline., US Book

g1443, **Great Cricket Betting Scandal**, Ted Corbett, £7.99pb, 209pp, This is an entertaining novel concerned with the mystery of the Indian sub-continent and the mysterious ways of their (illegal) bookmakers., UK Book

SPREAD BETTING

g1035, **Spread Betting To Win**, Jacques Black, £9.99pb, 164pp, Excellent primer to spread betting for novice and the more experienced better. Covers both sporting and financial markets. ALL LEVELS. 164 pages, UK Book

g1060, **Spread Betting**, Andrew Burke, £8.95pb, 192pp,   Written by Odds On columnist, this details all the basics of SB and then goes on to examine more complex areas such as value, risk, and how to form markets, UK Book

g1175, **Successful Spread Betting**, Geoff Harvey, £12.95pb, 158pp, Covers: spot 'value' in SB, win from arbitration opportunities, manage your account, understand spread psychology, and analyse SB markets. Covers football, golf, greyhounds, financial markets, UK Book

g1201, **Market Speculating**, Andrew Burke, £8.95pb, 157pp, A ground breaking book about how to Use spread betting on the financial markets. Explores the principle markets and offers essential advice for all investors. We're selling a lot of this, UK Book

g2020, **How To Win At Spread Betting**, Victor Knight, £4.95pb, 64pp, Pocket book. Useful beginners guide for this area of growing interest, UK Book

SMARTSIG

SMARTsig is a popular monthly magazine that we stock at High Stakes. Below are the contents from the last twelve issues of the magazine if you want to order one of the back issues listed please add the code number and date e.g. 7.06 Jun 2000 to the order form. Postage will be charge at £0.50 per issue Each issue costs £4.25

7.06 Jun 2000
Up Front – A Fool and His Money
Barbed Wire Betting
The Punter's Revenge XXI
Go To The Dogs For Value
I Hate Computers
Bias 2000... New Book extracts
Is Each-Way Betting Worthwhile?
KISS The Favourite Five
KISS Just Watch I'll Show 'Em
Golf – Ratings, One Size Fits All?
Remember the Bottom Lines!
The Ups and Downs of Share Trading
Know Your (Racing Post) Tipsters

7.07 July 2000
Up Front – Gone Fishin'
Avoiding Whiplash
Golf Value Betting
The Punter's Revenge Final Instalment
PSSSST! – Wanna a Free £50 Bet?
Tipsters, Value, Reality, Overnight Success
The Effects of Weight on AW Racing
Draw Bias, Tricasts & Trifectas
Horserace Spread Betting
KISS Five Day Method Update
KISS Horses for Courses
Profits From Racing

7.08 Aug 2000
Up Front – The Armchair Coach
Enhancement Through Staking
Essential Football Betting Guide
A winning System Using Internet
Proportional Staking
Enhancing Golf Profits
KISS Verily, it Came to Pass
KISS Topspeed System
Increase Win Chances Using Perms
Forecasts Are the Answer

Racing Post Topspeed
KISS 5-Year –old Handicappers

7.12 Dec 2000
Up Front – The World Moves On
Going, Going …. Gone
The TurfTrax Revolution
Early Odds Versus SP
Commercial Horses-To-Follow Lists
Soccer Superiority Spreads
Fancy 4/1 About An 11/4 Shot?
Only OneTip – But Napped
Watching The Tipsters
A Chance In A Million
Enthusiastic For Archie?
Official Handicap Ratings
Handicap Bottom Weights Re-Visit

8.01 Jan 2001
Up Front – Start The New Year Well
Commercial Horses-to-Follow Lists
Bookmaker Over-Rounds
Soccer Superiority Spreads
SMARTsig AW Ratings Revisited
Return On Investment, A Better Way
SMARTsig Full Index to Volume Seven
National Hunt Trainers Review
Hull City, First Half Champions
Lessons of the Lottery
A Process of Elimination
Minimise The Losing Runs

8.02 Feb 2001
www.wonderiftheyllstillbeherein6months.com
Archie Looks At Form
New Year Football Predictions
Price Wisely, Bet Wisely
Sample Race Analysis
Young Handicap Chasers
Handicap Weights
Trainers by Favourites and Courses
Commercial Horses-To-Follow Lists
Football superiority Spreads
Race Value and Class
KISS – Computer straight Forecasts
Blackjack Counting Phenomenon

8.03 March 2001
Up Front – Something's Stirring

86

Betabet Consortium
Betfair Betting Exchange
Betting – 2001 Style
Trainers & Favourites by Course II
Backing Multiple Selections
Doing Business On the Internet
Class Will Tell
D'alembert Staking
Computers That play Poker
Ignorance Is Bliss!
Extracts From BIAS 2001
Review – Football Betting To Win
Blackjack Counting Phenomenon II
Happy Birthday Tipping Comp
Soccer Superiority Spreads
Horses To Follow Update

8.04 April 2001
Up Front – Wouldn't You Just Know It!
Extracts From Bias 2001
Betting With Gay Abandon
Diary of a Rookie Pro
Trainers/Favourite for Courses III
The Hillman Plan
System Peaks & Troughs
Shhhhh! The "V" Word
Mug Punter or Value Hunter?
Too Many Assumptions
Horses To Follow Update
Soccer Superiority Spreads
Race Class & All – Weather Favourites

ORDER FORM

1) Enter the titles of the books you require along with their product number (e.g. 1035 SPREAD BETTING TO WIN), the quantity you require and the price on the order form overleaf.

2) Total the price at the bottom of the order form and add P&P as follows: UK - £1.95 plus 50p a book (e.g. 3 books would cost £1.95 + 3 x £0.50 [£1.50] - a total of £3.45) and elsewhere - £2.95 plus £1 a book (e.g. 2 books would cost £2.95 + 2 x £1 [£2] - a total of £4.95)

3) Cheque or postal orders must be in pounds sterling and be drawn on a UK bank and should be payable to High Stakes. If you prefer you can pay be credit card - just fill out the details below.

4) Send your completed order to: High Stakes Bookshop [cat2001], 21 Gt Ormond St, London, WC1N 3JB. You can fax credit card orders on 020 7430 0021 or you can also use our internet bookshop at www.highstakes. co.uk, which has secure ordering facilities.

We try and dispatch all orders for books that are in stock the same day but inevitably there are delays when a book is not available or has gone out of print. We will always endeavour to inform you of any lengthy delays.

N.B. Please ensure you fill in your address details below.

Name:

Address:

Postcode:

Tel No:

e-mail address:

Credit Card type:

Credit Card number:

Expiry date:

Issue No (if using Switch):

Start Date:

Signature (if paying by credit card):

ORDER FORM

Qty	Ref	Title	Cost
....	....	....	....
....	....	....	....
....	....	....	....
....	....	....	....
....	....	....	....
....	....	....	....
....	....	....	....
....	....	....	....
....	....	....	....
....	....	....	....
....	....	....	....

Sub Total ....

P&P ....

TOTAL ....

Have you remembered to include your name, address and cheque (if required) payable to: High Stakes

Send completed order form to: High Stakes [Cat2001], 21 Great Ormond St, London, WC1N 3JB

ORDER FORM

1) Enter the titles of the books you require along with their product number (e.g. 1035 SPREAD BETTING TO WIN), the quantity you require and the price on the order form overleaf.

2) Total the price at the bottom of the order form and add P&P as follows: UK - £1.95 plus 50p a book (e.g. 3 books would cost £1.95 + 3 x £0.50 [£1.50] - a total of £3.45) and elsewhere - £2.95 plus £1 a book (e.g. 2 books would cost £2.95 + 2 x £1 [£2] - a total of £4.95)

3) Cheque or postal orders <u>must be in pounds sterling and be drawn on a UK bank</u> and should be payable to High Stakes. If you prefer you can pay be credit card - just fill out the details below.

4) Send your completed order to: High Stakes Bookshop [cat2001], 21 Gt Ormond St, London, WC1N 3JB. You can fax credit card orders on 020 7430 0021 or you can also use our internet bookshop at www.highstakes. co.uk, which has secure ordering facilities.

We try and dispatch all orders for books that are in stock the same day but inevitably there are delays when a book is not available or has gone out of print. We will always endeavour to inform you of any lengthy delays.

N.B. Please ensure you fill in your address details below.

Name:

Address:

Postcode:

Tel No:

e-mail address:

Credit Card type:

Credit Card number:

Expiry date:

Issue No (if using Switch):

Start Date:

Signature (if paying by credit card):

ORDER FORM

Qty	Ref	Title	Cost
....	....	....	....
....	....	....	....
....	....	....	....
....	....	....	....
....	....	....	....
....	....	....	....
....	....	....	....
....	....	....	....
....	....	....	....
....	....	....	....
....	....	....	....

Sub Total ....

P&P ....

TOTAL ....

Have you remembered to include your name, address and cheque (if required) payable to: High Stakes

Send completed order form to: High Stakes [Cat2001], 21 Great Ormond St, London, WC1N 3JB

ORDER FORM

1) Enter the titles of the books you require along with their product number (e.g. 1035 SPREAD BETTING TO WIN), the quantity you require and the price on the order form overleaf.

2) Total the price at the bottom of the order form and add P&P as follows: UK - £1.95 plus 50p a book (e.g. 3 books would cost £1.95 + 3 x £0.50 [£1.50] - a total of £3.45) and elsewhere - £2.95 plus £1 a book (e.g. 2 books would cost £2.95 + 2 x £1 [£2] - a total of £4.95)

3) Cheque or postal orders <u>must be in pounds sterling and be drawn on a UK bank</u> and should be payable to High Stakes. If you prefer you can pay be credit card - just fill out the details below.

4) Send your completed order to: High Stakes Bookshop [cat2001], 21 Gt Ormond St, London, WC1N 3JB. You can fax credit card orders on 020 7430 0021 or you can also use our internet bookshop at www.highstakes. co.uk, which has secure ordering facilities.

We try and dispatch all orders for books that are in stock the same day but inevitably there are delays when a book is not available or has gone out of print. We will always endeavour to inform you of any lengthy delays.

N.B. Please ensure you fill in your address details below.

Name:

Address:

Postcode:

Tel No:

e-mail address:

Credit Card type:

Credit Card number:

Expiry date:

Issue No (if using Switch):

Start Date:

Signature (if paying by credit card):

ORDER FORM

Qty	Ref	Title	Cost
....	....	....	....
....	....	....	....
....	....	....	....
....	....	....	....
....	....	....	....
....	....	....	....
....	....	....	....
....	....	....	....
....	....	....	....
....	....	....	....
....	....	....	....
....	....	....	....

Sub Total ....

P&P ....

TOTAL ....

Have you remembered to include your name, address and cheque (if required) payable to: High Stakes

Send completed order form to: High Stakes [Cat2001], 21 Great Ormond St, London, WC1N 3JB

ORDER FORM

1) Enter the titles of the books you require along with their product number (e.g. 1035 SPREAD BETTING TO WIN), the quantity you require and the price on the order form overleaf.

2) Total the price at the bottom of the order form and add P&P as follows: UK - £1.95 plus 50p a book (e.g. 3 books would cost £1.95 + 3 x £0.50 [£1.50] - a total of £3.45) and elsewhere - £2.95 plus £1 a book (e.g. 2 books would cost £2.95 + 2 x £1 [£2] - a total of £4.95)

3) Cheque or postal orders <u>must be in pounds sterling and be drawn on a UK bank</u> and should be payable to High Stakes. If you prefer you can pay be credit card - just fill out the details below.

4) Send your completed order to: High Stakes Bookshop [cat2001], 21 Gt Ormond St, London, WC1N 3JB. You can fax credit card orders on 020 7430 0021 or you can also use our internet bookshop at www.highstakes. co.uk, which has secure ordering facilities.

We try and dispatch all orders for books that are in stock the same day but inevitably there are delays when a book is not available or has gone out of print. We will always endeavour to inform you of any lengthy delays.

N.B. Please ensure you fill in your address details below.

Name:

Address:

Postcode:

Tel No:

e-mail address:

Credit Card type:

Credit Card number:

Expiry date:

Issue No (if using Switch):

Start Date:

Signature (if paying by credit card):

ORDER FORM

Qty	Ref	Title	Cost
....	....	....	....
....	....	....	....
....	....	....	....
....	....	....	....
....	....	....	....
....	....	....	....
....	....	....	....
....	....	....	....
....	....	....	....
....	....	....	....
....	....	....	....
....	....	....	....

Sub Total ....

P&P ....

TOTAL ....

Have you remembered to include your name, address and cheque (if required) payable to: High Stakes

Send completed order form to: High Stakes [Cat2001], 21 Great Ormond St, London, WC1N 3JB